with Xmas greetings
from his father.
Hartford, Xmas 1915

The William Brewster Clark
Memorial Lectures
1913

The William Brewster Clark
Memorial Lectures
1913

THE RELIGIOUS REVOLUTION
OF TO-DAY

BY

JAMES T. SHOTWELL, Ph.D.

PROFESSOR OF HISTORY AT COLUMBIA UNIVERSITY
AND WILLIAM BREWSTER CLARK LECTURER
AT AMHERST COLLEGE FOR 1913

BOSTON AND NEW YORK
HOUGHTON MIFFLIN COMPANY
The Riverside Press Cambridge
1913

COPYRIGHT, 1913, BY JAMES T. SHOTWELL

ALL RIGHTS RESERVED

Published October 1913

TO

M. S.

FOREWORD

THE unique characteristic of modern times — one which gives every indication of being permanent — is that the world, both personal and external, is to an apparently increasing degree in a state of change. The immense significance of this fact is as yet but dimly perceived. The new modifies the old or displaces it in every department of life without exception and with increasing rapidity. New ideas, new movements, new ways of looking at things present themselves for attention for the first time or call upon people to change their attitude towards things they had considered settled. This state of the world renders the practical problems of personal conduct and social policy increasingly vital and complex, and makes the task of a college in its relation to them as much more difficult as an institution is less mobile than an individual.

To assist Amherst College, therefore, in throwing light in a genuinely scientific spirit upon the relation of the research, discovery, and thought of the day to individual attitude and social policy is our aim in the foundation of these lectures. Such light may come through a recent discovery in natural or applied science, through a new tendency in art, literature, or music; it may be the result of some painstaking research in history or anthropology; or it may be found in some vital movement, religious, philosophic, economic, or political. It is our wish that men and women who are in the position of leaders in such phases of the life of the day shall give to Amherst College and the world an exposition of their particular work in its relation to what they conceive to be a modern outlook.

We give these lectures in memory of William Brewster Clark, M.D., who graduated from Amherst in the class of 1876. We believe that no place for a memorial to him could be more fitting than the college which he loved with a devotion characteristically rich and sincere, nor any form more suitable than lectures on subjects which to him would be most absorbing.

FANNY H. CLARK,
W. EVANS CLARK.

NEW YORK CITY, 11 March, 1913.

CONTENTS

I. CONTRASTS 1

II. DEVOLUTION OR EVOLUTION? 41

III. THE PROBLEM AND THE DATA 82

IV. THE NEW RÉGIME 121

THE RELIGIOUS REVOLUTION OF TO-DAY

I

CONTRASTS

We are in the midst of a religious revolution! The "old régime" of immemorial belief and custom is vanishing before our eyes. Faiths so old that they come to us from the prehistoric world are yielding to the discoveries of yesterday. Institutions that have embodied these faiths and held the allegiance of the civilized world are now crumbling to pieces or transforming themselves wherever the new forces of the revolution touch and penetrate. The brand of superstition is being placed upon many of the most cherished beliefs of our fathers. The authority of our venerable orthodoxies, seemingly so securely centered in inspiration, and once so emphatically asserted in creeds, is now assailed from within and without. We are reconstructing the ancient realm in which they ruled. Reason and science, which are our ideals, however irrational and unscientific we are, are changing the frontiers of thought. We find in them rather than in the acceptance of orthodox dogma, the clue to what gives direction to our society to-day,— invention, politics, modern art and literature, the concentration of our energies upon the conquest of the material world, psychology at work upon the laws of behavior instead of an adjunct to theology, biology with its suggestions of a mechanistic universe, philosophy turning from scholasticism of various forms to the interpretation of science, and the new realization of the economic basis of most social movements, even of most morality. All these complex phenomena of the outlook of to-day are acquisitions of the secular spirit. They may have religion in them; but it is not the old religion. Indeed, where in their midst the old religion still resides, it generally stands out by its contrast; and its field is narrowing steadily. Their growth overshadows it on many sides, cutting off superstitions and transforming theologies; and they are managing their own affairs without its interference.

The revolution is as sudden as it is vast. I myself have lived in the two régimes. I am tolerably sure, moreover, that some before me now are living in one, some in the other. To be sure, like all great movements it was long in preparation, and much was done before the world awakened to it. But now the alarm of the old and the triumph of the new are obvious to any one who looks at either side. I cannot find in any church where there is a congregation of average intelligence the preacher who will deliver the sermons of my boyhood. As for the sermons that deal with the disturbed and disappearing faiths, and reinterpret the old dogmas to mean something new, — I can hardly escape them, if I go to church at all. It is only, however, when one recalls that the sermons of his boyhood were those of all the ages, that one realizes what the revolution means. For from Augustine to Timothy Dwight the fundamentals of religion remained practically unchanged. Now Dwight is classed, along with Cotton Mather, as a historical curiosity, a specimen in the museum of thought, and only the prodigious grasp of Augustine's philosophy and his historic importance in the building-up of the Christian doctrine secure for him a place in our curricula. A new era has dawned in the history of human thought.

Let me interrupt myself here to say that I am not here to preach the revolution! I am merely attempting to state it. The historian, as Polybius so emphatically asserted, must be no partisan. "Directly a man assumes the moral attitude of a historian, he ought to forget all considerations such as love of one's friends, hatred of one's enemies. . . . He must sometimes praise enemies and blame friends. For as a living creature is rendered useless if deprived of its eyes, so if you take truth from history, what is left but an idle and unprofitable tale."[1] This is the simple ideal of scientific history, but from Polybius to Macaulay the bias in even the master historians has shown how difficult this simple ideal really is. It is not so very hard, perhaps, to recognize the good in one's enemies, and certainly not to stop battling for one's friends. But the difficulty is to divest one's self of prejudices, whose very existence we scarcely suspect. This is what makes the study of religion so treacherous. Here even the clearest eye is likely to

[1] Book I, chap. 14.

trace the perspectives through the warping glass of prejudice. Indeed, some distortion is inevitable, for the glass is before the eye of us all. Let me ask you frankly to put the question to yourselves whether, even the few statements I have already made, have not already aroused your prejudices! The very assertion that there is a religious revolution seems to most of us like an invitation to take sides. Some of you are, I am perfectly sure, already framing arguments against the sweeping generalization with which I began; some of you are giving it a mental nod of approval. Each side sees that the attitude of the other is unscientific; but it is hard for us to realize that both are equally so. Now unless we overcome this innate tendency, — you as well as I, — we may as well not take up the problems before us at all. For we shall have them all solved before we touch them. We must learn not to care for whatever has meant most to us, — excepting only the truth; and we shall find truth only upon that wide-open but almost untraveled road which leads away from ourselves.

With this caution in mind let us return to our problem, which is not to prove the existence of a religious revolution,— for that is admitted by all who give the situation any thought, and is the starting-point for almost every treatment of the place of religion in modern life, — but to measure its importance and see its setting in the history of the world. It is not a problem in theology but in the social sciences; in anthropology, psychology, sociology and history. We are not concerned with whether things ought to be so or not, but with what they are and have been. The truth or falseness of this or that doctrine lies outside the story of its rôle in human history, and we are dealing with our problem from the human side. We see religion shifting its place in society and wish to learn how deep the change has gone, how lasting it is likely to prove and what is its setting in the evolution of civilization. This involves a consideration of belief, too, but only as a social phenomenon, embodying changing attitudes. Religion is so much a thing of belief that it is impossible to go beneath the surface of its institutions without entering to some degree into its myths or theologies. But just as one can treat the influence of the Monroe Doctrine upon American history, discover its origins historically and interpret in its light the spirit of American diplomacy, without settling the question of its justice, so one can pass in review the changing field of religious belief, and in a purely historical survey, watch the movement of revolutionary disturbance which dominates there now. The problem is historical in the truest sense; as genuinely historical as the decline of the Roman Empire or the rise of democracy. To be sure history has seldom been realized in so wide a synthesis, involving every one of the social sciences, and there are those who object to setting such tasks for a mere muse like Clio. But history is no longer a tale for the credulous; it is the coöperative record of the evolution of our civilization, and it must cover the data of every phase to learn the real significance of any.

What follows, then, is a survey of such facts, or rather a summary of them, since the evidence is too vast to be presented in any one series of lectures, however long. It already fills libraries, and is only begun. Much of it deals with the unhistoric and the uncivilized. For, as biology seeks light upon the nature of life in a study of the lower organisms, and psychology is watching the twitches of protoplasm through microscopes to learn the meaning of our own behavior, so anthropology has found in primitive societies a key to the meaning of the culture of the civilized and sociology is applying the key. The result has been a new understanding, not simply of the present, but of all history. The story of the evolution of society is now being worked out by a great coöperative effort of scientists, some in the heart of Africa or Australia, others digging in the hills of Crete, others again testing the texts of the Bible against the background of Asian paganism, gathering the evidence of folk-lore and folk-ways in secluded villages, or watching, through the mass of accumulated evidence in our libraries, law emerge from priestcraft and reason from the trammels of mythology.

We turn, then, to this composite survey for light upon the present situation, to see if it can clarify the outlook or explain the meaning of the change which is taking place to-day, a change so fundamental that it seems to imply the overturn of the whole trend of past philosophy and the destruction of institutions as old as all civilization. But these historical and anthropological sciences, when interrogated upon so vital a matter as the place of religion in society, instead of offering at once a cleared perspective, in which the changing present takes its place definitely and shows its significance by contrast with the past, reveal a view of religious history which comes with as startling surprise as the discovery of the present revolution itself to one who has just learned to see it. For they show that the scope of religion in society has been declining all along the ages, from the primitive world to ours. The religious revolution of to-day, viewed from the standpoint of all the past, turns out to be but a swifter phase of an age-long movement, — and the history of civilization itself is a history of secularization. From the world of the primitive to that of the modern, the progress of culture has gone side by side with a lessening of what we now term superstition, but was once religion, and a steady growth of purely secular control.

This is not to say that the amount of religion decreases as society advances. The social sciences are not in a position to make any statement upon that point. What is lost in extent may be gained in intensity. We shall deal with that later. But whether religion is less or more, its field of action and its authority are steadily being more and more circumscribed. Once one has had one's eyes opened to the nature of primitive society, and so realizes what elements history started with, — the paralyzing superstitions, the dominance of magic, the persistent taboo, the luck or curse in men and things, — then one begins to realize that a story of emancipation means at the same time a rejection of authority, — a point one is likely to forget. To the student of social evolution who approaches his question with fresh and untrammeled mind, there is no larger fact in the history of mankind than this narrowing of the sphere of religion, and none more remarkable than the failure to recognize it until anthropology took us outside ourselves. For now we see that the process of civilization means that society is assuming control of itself, making its own the world it once shared with superstition, facing undaunted the things of its former fears, and so carving out for itself, from the realm of mystery in which it lies, a sphere of unhampered action and a field of independent thought.

The religious revolution, then, seems to have come as the last, swift phase of an age-long movement, — at least so the anthropologist product of Brahmanism; Chinese conservatism and Japanese solidarity are alike rooted in the worship of the dead. And these beliefs are as vital to-day as the institutions they create are strong. To be sure, faith varies there as here, but as science has given its tone to the thought — even the religion — of the modern West, so the East as a whole stands for religion and admits its preëminent claims. Now and again Hindoo or Chinese reformers have lightened the burden of its authority and emphasized the claims of reason and simple morality. Such were Buddha and Confucius. But although there was the promise of emancipation in their ideals, they have won but a limited allegiance and have been for the most part lost or distorted in the superstitions they combated. They have suffered the fate which generally befalls the man who reforms from within. The saint or prophet who protests is himself, in course of time, added to that very pantheon against which he fulminated. For however the gods come and go, their caravansary is always full. The worship of ancestors, with its sacrifices and its magic, lies deeper at the roots of patriarchal China than the reforming precepts of Confucius. Brahmanism, which

Buddha would have purified, far from dead, is one of the most vital forces in the world to-day. We have but little idea of its continual spread through the hills and jungles of India, among the non-Aryan and casteless tribes, engulfing, as Lyall says, like an ocean, the ever-breaking shore of primitive beliefs which mark the ethnical frontiers of the Hindoo. What a spectacle of skepticism we offer to races like these, where religion really counts. If we could see the world in terms of religion, we might appreciate what it would mean to have "foreign devils" defile our temples, and see reasons for an Indian mutiny.

The East has seen us in the same contrasted light as we see it. We stand for material and rational triumphs, and it is this phase of our culture which it appropriates. In the meeting of East and West, one might think that those Oriental nations which had treasured faith and ritual so long and so intensely, whose ideal rests so largely upon the promises of immortality, would have chosen from the gifts of the West the religion we offer, and ignored the rest. But they ask for science rather than for Christianity.

The significance of this seems to escape us.

It indicates the relative activity of our own religious and secular forces. It shows us what elements are mainly at work in the spread of European civilization. The onward march of that culture sums up for most of us what we call progress, and its conquest, not of the Orient only, but of the whole world, now in mid-career, forms the most tremendous spectacle in the annals of mankind. Yet, in spite of heroic missionaries on the frontier lines, in spite of *Te Deums* for victories in Arabian seas, it is a triumph of secularization. It is sacrilege, backed by the most potent forces the world has known, — nor merely by British fleets or German armies, but by the irresistible might of rationalized industry and modern science. Before these forces the dreamy East is giving up her dreams; the factory whistle is breaking in upon the clanking of the pagoda bells; the muezzin's call to prayer yields to the more imperious call to work. Religion was the heritage of the Orient; science the achievement of the West; and the West is the victor. It, too, of course, has its religion to offer, but not of a kind to hinder industry and commerce, and not even — at present at least — to block rationalism.

So when the West meets the East, the result, so far as one can see it in the aims of the society which their meeting engenders, is not that there is added more religion to the wealth of customs and beliefs which gives the tone to those arrested civilizations. It may change some of the currents of those customs and beliefs and vitalize some of their possibilities by a change of emphasis and a new center for their reverence. But these are hardly more than by-products. The converts to Christianity are few compared with the converts to science. The taboos are not merely changing their sanction, they are breaking down. Science through its inventions has got might upon its side as well. It has armed the revolution which ended the Manchu dynasties of China. The new republic is to be ruled, not through an appeal to ancestors, but after the model of England and America, where the power of the purse in the House of Commons has secularized for all practical purposes the divine right of kings, or where law is created at the direct behest of business and the constitution recognizes no taboos. The claims of reason as against those of tradition and authority are stirring with portentous movement in the tranquil, religious depths of four hundred million people. In Japan the new era has already dawned, and even India is at last showing the signs of an industrial as well as national awakening.

The Industrial Revolution has reached the Orient. The political and social history of the Far East at present must be read in the light of that underlying fact. It is the new industrial Japan which is throwing its colonies across the Pacific and pushing into Asia; it was the industrial south of China which bred the recent revolution. Even in India the new national consciousness is bound up with the practical appliances of modern science. There is, therefore, something deeper before us than a mere political readjustment. Beneath the political there is a social and beneath the social a religious readjustment, — a breaking-up of world-old customs and beliefs. Caste is broken in upon in India when a common railway carriage is used by all and a city is forced to fall back upon a common waterworks system. The contact that defiles is now unavoidable, and so it ceases to defile. Brahmans, who maintained their sacred isolation for centuries in the static conditions of the past, are accommodating themselves to the dynamics of Western civilization. When Chinese families are torn apart for mills and offices and scattered as ours have been, who will tend the ancestors' tombs? The old loyalty will not at once disappear; the Shinto worship has roots too deep to be torn up in a single generation. But that it is bound to yield before the forces of the West,—the scientific forces mainly, —no one who has watched the process of recent Oriental history can doubt for a moment.

The East, the static East, is dissolving at our touch. But it still remains a monument of what we might have been, — and indeed narrowly escaped becoming. It furnishes us a contrast which helps us to see what we really have become.

Turn now to the savage and compare his world with ours. As the East shows the possibilities of religious culture which we have never attained, and which our rationalism frankly rejects, the savage shows what society is like when well-nigh devoid of that rationalism altogether. His science is magic, his morals taboos; religion saturates his emotions, dictates his etiquette, governs behavior and thought, and determines his society. It is the same the world over, with merely local variations. Not only are there no savage people known to us who are without religion, but the more they are investigated the more their customs and institutions appear rooted in it. It begins with the processes of generation and presides over birth; under its auspices the child acquires manhood, and from it he learns his duties to society; life is passed amid its prescriptions; it can be faced only with its own inventions, for its sanction is death. Death is not a natural, but a supernatural event, as it still seems to be with most of us. Irresistible, omnipotent, armed with the destiny of men, religion — including magic — alone can supply the "medicines" for the evils it brings. It holds the secret of pain, — in crystals, in malignant bones, in passings of the hand that has held things sacred or accursed, in stars, in voices of the wind. It literally runs in the blood, the sight of which may transfix with superstitious terror, — the medium of sacrament, the essential in sacrifice the world over. Its omens direct affairs of state, through the hooting of an owl or the howl of a wolf, or the stumbling of a warrior.[1] The most trivial incidents thus acquire tremendous importance, and furnish a clue to the future and a guide for the present. One must observe the minutest regulations or suffer the results in droughts or storms or plagues or accidents.

It is unnecessary to insist upon this all-embracing rôle of religion in primitive life. Books on anthropology are full of it, and of little else. Religion is the background against which rise the outlines of society. It is the first science, philosophy and art of mankind. Abundant illustration of this is at hand for all who care to find it. In the light of such a contrast our Christian civilization shows its religious limitations.

This is not to say that the savage has *more* religion than the Christian. That is not the question; but in any case he has more in relation to other things. It more largely fills his life. But then again that does not mean that his life is full.

The actions and outlook of the savage may

---

[1] Stubbing one's toe on the warpath means defeat. William the Conqueror is said to have fallen on the beach at Pevensey, but he rose, like a good rationalist, with a handful of sand, to show that he had done it on purpose.

be dominated by religion without his being eternally lost in a religious atmosphere, like an Indian Yogi or a mediæval monk. He is not generally bothered about atmospheres at all. So long as life runs along normally he is the most unreligious animal in human form. A savage does not spend his life in constant terror of his lurking demons, chattering his magic spells at every opportunity; nor is he eternally conscious of the taboos which thwart him in chase or war. He does not meditate upon these things as we might, simply because he is not much given to meditating upon anything. It would be wrong to say that he does not meditate at all, but he has not acquired the habit of self-examination to the same extent as we have. To be sure the savage is not the simple-minded creature anthropologists used to make him out to be, and we are finding more puzzling depths in him the more we acquire the possibility of viewing the world in his way. But after all, his thought is not so persistent, so voluntary, so capable of direction as ours, for in this discipline of the mind lies about the only difference we can see between ourselves and him. So, although capable of much control where we often lack it, his mind seems to keep no active concentration on these religious phenomena which form his world. Thought, like emotion, is with him mostly a response to some stimulus from without — and to maintain its attitude effectively only when the stimulus still is active. It is something like a lingering echo in the cells of the brain of a call from without, that thrills and dies, or like the confused register of waves of light and color, as the light changes and the colors fade. Thought, therefore, in general, shares at first both the direction and the attitudes of emotion. Primitive thinking is intermittent and mostly involuntary, as is, after all, mostly the case with us, too. There is much of our own time when we can hardly be said to think; instinct and habit are more important still than reason. Their somnorific influences continue to make life possible and enjoyable even, as reason grows more conscious and science more sure of the insignificance of its rôle in the grim tragedy of the universe. So with the savage; instinct and habit render his world of potential terrors much more comfortable than we might think. His thought is caught where attention draws it, mainly through events of surprise or danger, or crises, and if fixed at all, fixed through the continuity of joint stimulation upon things of importance to himself or the tribe. It is only in such circumstances that savages attain any acute, or perhaps even any measurable, "awareness" of themselves or their environment. To be sure such strains of attention may spill over, as it were, into the more normal run of daily life, and the spilt product may persist in habit long after the original attention or stimulus has passed away. But it is the strain on the nerves which first tingles with the activity of thought.

For the sake of clarity we have spoken of this awakening of thought as if it were the product of individual brains. But it is by way of the group, the horde, or tribe that the individual first acquires consciousness. Thought is too intimately associated with expression to flourish by itself, unexpressed, in the dark recesses of a primitive brain. There its images apparently lack the continuity and variety which mutual exchange and comparison enable them to acquire. Thought is a thing of the camp-fire, of gesture and speech. It needs more than the stimulation to attention to a single passing experience; it must be approached from more than one angle in order to disentangle it from the confusion of momentary impressions of reality. The experience may have to be repeated and worked over until its significance is borne home, — and in some of the largest facts of life that cannot be done by the individual, since he dies in the experiment. In any case, consciousness develops first in and through the group. It is from such experiences in which he shares that the individual learns to appropriate for himself lessons of conduct from the common store and so through the confusion of his own reactions to gain a personal basis for independent judgment or thought. To be sure, before he has done this, it is a little premature to talk of thought at all; for the best the group can do is to socialize its emotions and learn how to meet the situations in which they arise.

Now it is just these objects of group emotional apprehension, which are the objects of primitive religion. The more attention is concentrated upon anything, the greater emotional disturbance it awakens, and the more it calls for adjustment. In this emotional strain and sensing of things lies the core of religion. It is not too much to say that thought and religion, rooted alike in emotion, are at least complementary, if not, indeed, coterminous in the earliest outlook of humanity.

To many this seems mere guesswork. No one has assisted at such dim beginnings and brought us any account of them. Comparative psychology is still in its infancy; anthropology has never found a primitive man; it deals with societies of long and important culture even in the lowest savages it finds. Yet all the evidence we have points in one direction. The further we penetrate, the less we find of savage society which lacks the imprint of religion. And it is particularly those things which are of vital concern to the tribe, upon which, therefore, its attention must have been especially concentrated, which perpetuate in greatest degree that elemental religious stamp. Birth and death, — of prime importance, not to the individual, who is unconscious of their operation, but to the tribe or family whose existence is affected by them, — adolescence, by which the tribe gains a warrior or a potential parent, marriage which holds the relations of the groups in permanence, or crises of less normal occurrence, such as war and the chase

— these are phenomena which universally and without question develop the situations which bear the stamp of the taboo.[1] It may be only the stamp, for the process of secularization is as old as progress. But luckily for the scientist, although unfortunately for his savage predecessors, the stamp is nigh ineradicable. Fixed in the habits and perpetuated by unconscious repetition long after their origins are lost to mind, such imprints of prehistoric religious emotions lie thick on every institution which reaches back to primitive society. And so, although we can never find the really primitive society itself, we have in institutions and customs, and in that earliest embodiment of human outlook into this strange world, mythology, evidences of things immeasurably older than even their own origins.

In contrast with savage society, ours, outwardly at least, is frankly profane. Moreover, here, as in the Orient, the touch of the West means secularization. The spectacle of the white man raising good crops without reli-

[1] There are many other bases for taboo, naturally. We are following merely a relatively simplified line of thought in order not to lose sight of the problem before us in a mass of details.

CONTRASTS

gious ceremonies, which disturbed the foundations of the Pueblo Indians' moral universe, is the kind of thing that destroys religion most effectively; and the white man cannot move without violating such taboos. Natives themselves soon become his ally. Those in touch with whites are burning to assert the superiority which this gives them and hence pooh-hoo their former ceremonies — not perhaps without some secret qualms. Physicians, traders, and missionaries are at one here. Before them the fetishes disappear and the gods die. The process has never been better described than by that Zulu quoted by Bishop Calloway. Once Unkulunkulu was a very great god of the Zulus. The white man settled on the veldt broke his laws, violated his sacred rituals, and now (says the Zulu) his name "is like the name of a very old crone, which has not the power to do even a little thing for herself, but sits continually where she sat in the morning till the sun sets. And the children make sport of her, for she cannot catch and flog them, but only talk with her mouth. Just so is the name of Unkulunkulu."[1] The frailty of what was once omnip-

[1] Cf. Tylor, *Primitive Culture*, II, 285. The incident is frequently quoted.

otent has never been better phrased. Such gods are passing everywhere; how many there were and what rôle they played it will never be possible to say; for the stern march of progress obliterates even their monuments.

The history of antiquity offers us the same contrasts, if we care to see them. But if we care to see them we must come upon them from the other side — the primitive side; take account of the history before them rather than the history since. Afterwards, history arranges its canvas to suit what has since occurred. The texts of Christianity, for example, furnish but a slight idea of the intensity of the religious activity concentrated in the Egyptian or Oriental mysteries which it overcame. Who of us can appreciate antique paganism? The gods of Greece or Rome are for us hardly more than the mutilated statues of them in our museums, — pitiable, helpless objects before the scrutiny and comments of a passing crowd. Venus is an armless figure from the Louvre; Dionysos does not mean to us divine possession, the gift of tongues, or immortality; Attis brings no salvation. But to antiquity the "pagan" cults were no mockery. They were as real as Polynesian heathenism or Christianity to-day. That is something we can never quite realize, who have dwelt aloof with the poets and philosophers of antiquity or who see it athwart the Christian sources, in which the religion of the Jews stands out as the one genuine religion. "Paganism" was just as genuine as Judaism. It was a parallel development out of the same primal stuff, — or rather there were parallel developments, for there were all sorts of paganisms. Perhaps our perspective will never be clear so long as we talk of paganism at all. Viewed scientifically there was no such thing. There were merely a number of religions, of which the Jewish was one. The distinction is dogmatic, not one of essence. The non-Jewish, non-Christian cults were as various in kind as in vitality. As religions always do, they fitted themselves to their own societies, or rather the societies fitted them to themselves. Nor did the pagan cults die out suddenly, as many of our histories imply, like sickly, moribund things. They have lived on in our enlightened Europe to an extent perhaps equal to the Jewish beliefs which furnish the externals of orthodoxy. Here and there, within the Church and without it, in cults and folk-lore, in proverbs and taboos, the old religions still abide.

From the anthropological standpoint all antiquity was essentially alike, a vast magazine of variant developments from primitive stuff. The Jews emerge into history, not a nation of keen spiritual aspirations and altruistic ethics, but that pagan people, worshiping rocks, sheep and cattle, and spirits of caves and wells, of whom the Old Testament, tending towards its higher ideal, gives fragmentary but convincing evidence. The Romans, like the Jews, enter history with a vast supply of gods and demons. There were mysterious presences wherever one turned,—*numina*, vaguely personal but multitudinous. Later, the pontiffs gave them names and preserved, with some priestly elaboration, the lists of these uncanny sprites of the daily life. There were Abeona who protected the children when they first left the house, Domiduca who ordinarily brought them back, Interduca who guarded them on the way, Cunina who protected the child in the cradle while Cuba gave it sleep, Educa who taught it to eat, Fabulinus who taught it to speak, Statanus or Statina who taught it to stand, Levana who lifted it

up from the ground, etc. The husbandman
had Imporcitor to help him plow his furrows,
Insitor to sow the seeds, which themselves
had Seia while underground, Segetea when
showing above it, Nodutus when the stalk was
heading, Lacturnus when the kernel got milky.
Messia and Messor helped to cut the grain,
Convector and Conditor to bring it home and
mow it away, and Tutilina protected the barns
where it was stored. From these priestly for-
mulations one can catch a glimpse of the intense religious life of those peasant peoples
whose sacred fires were burning on the Etrus-
can and Campagnian hills centuries before the
myth of Romulus had even been imagined.
The old indigenous gods passed away as circumstances changed; but, as in India, the
pantheon was always full.

Religion in Rome was not a thing of poetic
myth, nor simply a mirror of the beauty or
mystery of nature. It was eminently practical,
and therefore eminently effective in both home
and state. As the word *religio* itself came to
suggest,[1] it was the expression of a moral tie,

[1] Fowler holds that it meant originally "the natural feeling of man in the presence of the supernatural," and that
the later meaning, "the feeling which suggests worship and

of duty and social obligation, from which, as from its own auguries, one might foretell the political bent of its people. But politics and religion were one. The city-state itself, that cell of the structure of antique society, was a product of their fusion. The king was a pontiff as well as a war-lord; the magistrate had his duties first toward the gods and then toward the people; law was sacred formula, patriotism was piety, and exile excommunication. The city walls were sacred limits for the gods, the city itself a sort of precinct of the temple which crowned the citadel. The shedding of blood within the city was sacrilege rather than crime; taboos of blood and death which rest upon all primitive warriors prevented its armies from entering its gates. The sacred hearth, whose little flame was the one thing that lived from forgotten centuries, was the feeble symbol of the immortality of social

the forms under which we perform that worship," was due to the need on the part of men like Lucretius and Cicero of a word which had not yet been appropriated as a technical term to express this idea. Cf. *Roman Religious Experience*, pp. 459, 460. As was suggested above, primitive peoples are not aware of religion in the widest sense, but only of its most striking aspects. This, however, does not imply that their religion is as restricted as their view of it. Most of primitive religion is dominated by action rather than by belief.

CONTRASTS

life. Time was measured in terms of holy days and their corresponding taboos and sacrifices, the round of whose observance marks the beginning of our calendar. "Sacra," which were once like the secrets of savage medicine men, remained to within historic times the sign and prerogative of patricians. Citizenship was itself religious. Even to the close of the republic, the magistrates were formally chosen by the gods through the auguries as well as by men; and a crash of thunder, as a sign from Jove, obliged the assemblies to adjourn until the next day. In the words of Fustel de Coulanges, "Law, government, and religion in Rome were three confused aspects of one thing."

The events of ancient history become intelligible only against this background. The will of " the gods " was the key to policies of state, and the first business of the magistracy was to find it out. The way a sacred chicken got a grain stuck in its throat would determine war or peace. Reforms voted through the assembly might be vetoed by a flash of lightning — visible to a reactionary magistrate. Campaigns were fought under the same uncertain leadership. Luckily the rest of the world ran their politics and made war on the same grounds. Hannibal, marching unchecked upon Rome after the battle of Cannæ, was turned back, only at the second milestone from Porta Capena on the Appian Way, by a voice in a dream. The Romans built upon the spot a shrine to the god Rediculus. Why not? He had saved Rome. His existence was evidenced by the recoil of the invincible Hannibal. Indeed, the whole current of Western history bears witness to it. The annals of Rome are full of such incidents, where the gods openly take control. But one gradually becomes suspicious of the amount of credit they receive. For the Roman made his religion so practical that he even undertook to direct the gods rather than they him. If they opposed his will, he had but to find the proper argument by way of sacrifice and propitiation to win them to his cause. If he gave enough and gave it under proper taboos, he could count — generally — upon divine acquiescence. The Calvinistic doctrine of predestination was turned the other way; the gods lost their free will! Or, viewed from another standpoint, in that confusion of religion and politics, politics effected a confused sort of secularization of religion itself.

This religious character of antique society has been obscured by two things, our rationalism, which makes us much more interested in the rational than in the irrational in history, and the limitations of our theological outlook.

In the first place we see antiquity in the light of its independent thinkers. Greece means to us, generally, the genius of Socrates, Plato and Aristotle, keen, bold criticism, the high achievement of thought and the foundations of science. It seldom suggests the haunting bogies of house and field, the rites of aversion by which the Greek, like the savage of to-day, got rid of the ill-luck that came from broken taboos, the howling fakirs who brought magic from the Orient, the Orphic orgies or the mysteries which drew thousands with their sacrificial pigs along the road from Athens to Eleusis. We see the world of a Pliny, credulous, magical, primitive, in terms of the keen analysis of a Lucretius or the common sense of a Cicero. The humanists of the Renaissance taught us to look that way, and ever since ancient history has kept to that perspective. But nothing could be more false than to read a whole history in terms of an enlightenment which was too weak to prevail in its own time. The antique victory of intellectual independence was a limited one, and it did not bring the emancipation of mankind. The career of superstition, which reaches from beyond Tertiary caves to the present, and in which Roman empires are but things of a day, was but little checked by Socrates or Aristotle. Philosophy itself was carried off to the mysteries or absorbed by Christian theologians. It was a religion, not a science, which presided over the fall of Rome. Had it been a science, Rome might not have fallen when it did.

If the rationalism of the humanists ignored the forces of paganism, theology derided them. It seemed absurd to attribute a real rôle to mere superstition. Superstition to the theologian is merely error; and error suggests futility. Who has not felt the subtle influence of that suggestion? Paganism does not amount to much if viewed as a false hypothesis, invented to cover the real facts, which are simply part of God's plan — a more or less negligible part, since the main scheme was worked out in Judea. And this is what it does amount to in the common Christian view. The scheme of world-history in general vogue for the last fifteen hundred years has maintained against paganism a successful conspiracy of silence.

This is not to say that the early Christians denied the reality of pagan gods. Not at all. They were as sure of that as of the reality of Christ. It was not until paganism passed outwardly away that other theologians interpreted it in that sense. Augustine places over against the City of God a City of Satan, so real, so swarming with gods and demons, so complete in its sovereignty over the lives of men, that it stands out in stronger realism, if less definite in outline, than that Divine City whose walls of spiritual peace he rears imaginatively upon the ruins of the old. Compared with the realities which he depicts and derides, the gorgeous creation of his imagination and faith is as unreal as it is sublime. The ancient city such as Fustel de Coulanges rediscovered for us, and which is slowly being reconstructed in the light of history and archæology, is simply that City of Satan denounced by Augustine.

We must reserve for our next lecture the treatment of Christianity itself. But we should miss the whole point of this study if we imagine that what we have been looking at is something apart from us, mere matter for detached curiosity. The Orient furnishes us a contrast, it is true; but savage and antique societies furnish chapters of our own history, chapters which are not yet closed. This is not simply a guessing hypothesis of an evolutionist; it is definitely proven.

We are learning from savagery the nature of civilization and from the stagnant East that of progress. The discovery of ourselves takes place from without. Just as the contrast with the antique culture opened up to the humanist of the Renaissance the possibility of a critical view of Christendom, so the new learning of to-day, whose classical speech is mainly the agglomerative grunts of savages, and whose philosophy was ancient when that of Socrates was young, is forcing upon us a similar and much more radical reconstruction. For the Renaissance of to-day comes in upon us from all sides.

Archæology is reconstructing the lost theater of history and anthropology refilling the stage. The long prelude to the *comédie humaine* is slowly being recovered. The actors had left nothing behind their darkened footlights but a few remains of the masks they wore and the tools they used, but their play survived. No classic tragedy can rank with its immortality. It is the drama of life in Australia or Africa to-day as it was in the prehistoric world. There are variations in details, but the acts and even the scenes have little changed. From birth to death, through adventure of chase or danger of war, through passions of love and hate and the crises that mark the change of acts, the mime of magic, religion, and custom continues in its primitive mould. Time is losing its old perspectives. The cave men are more real than Romulus.

We talk of the work of the humanists in the fifteenth and sixteenth centuries as a renaissance. They recovered the forgotten classics and enlarged the perspective of history to include the pagan world. It was an important service, an essential step in the emancipation of the intellect. But compared with the outlook of a humanist, the horizon of to-day has become almost infinite, and we bring to this larger knowledge instruments of analysis unknown before. We have acquired the elements of a scientific method, which the humanists lacked. Viewed from our standpoint of to-day, theirs was but another type of the mediæval mind. They did not get outside the mould of Western thought, but merely deplored what the schoolmen exalted and exalted what the schoolmen deplored. If, in spite of their limitations, the new knowledge which they brought was sufficient to restate the whole process of European history, to awaken a spirit of criticism which brought rationalism and science, the larger revelations of the renaissance of to-day will surely supply a new interpretation of ourselves. In the light of it, rightly or wrongly, the meaning of our civilization will be read.

II

DEVOLUTION OR EVOLUTION?

Our own past held all the possibilities of India. We started like any other savages. Somehow we do not see the full implication of this. The East is far away; savagery is farther still. Paganism is in another world from ours. We can view them and their history unmoved by any personal feelings. No straining of the imagination nor sense of scientific fact can ever make them quite our own. But when we turn to Christianity, at once we find ourselves alive to unsuspected emotions. We suddenly realize that the problem means us. Has the scope of our own religion been narrowing, too? It needs no trick of argument to bring this home and stir our interest, as it does when dealing with other religions and societies. We know it all too soon! So deep-seated is this sense of identification that we instinctively resent any criticism which seems unsympathetic, and eagerly seize upon any pretext for throwing it off the track. Just where impartiality is most needed we are generally unable to apply it. By a peculiar warp in our thinking, impartiality here seems like an attack. We accord to our religion what we call "sympathetic" or "constructive" criticism, by which too often is meant no criticism at all, but merely justification. It is the subtle turning of the apologist upon the critic, forcing him to drop his tools before he begins work. And we are all apologists. Few indeed are free from a sense of the possible impropriety of such speculations. For Christianity has placed such tremendous emphasis upon faith that any independent attitude in which the creations of faith are questioned, seems inherently hostile. The whole matter is at once thrown into an arena where anti-clerical and clerical, secular-minded and mystic, will applaud or jeer, not for what we are really doing, but because we seem to be hurting or helping one or the other side.

In the face of such a situation there is only one way to treat the problem of the historic rôle of Christianity. We can hardly expect even the most obvious facts to be accepted at their face value. For the facts of the past have as personal a tone as those of the present. The only way to handle them is to disown

DEVOLUTION OR EVOLUTION? 43

them. Treat discarded elements of religion as superstitions, — however real a part of religion they were in their own time and however integral a part they have been of the process of evolution, — and we may secure the same detached point of view for a survey of them as we have for the external world. The device is even likely to succeed too much, for we are apt to pride ourselves upon the process of denudation, and, regarding " superstitions" as always having been superstitions, see in their disappearance no real significance. That would be falsifying history on the other side. For most superstitions are past orthodoxies; even the worst of them were, in all probability, part of a genuine religion somewhere, some time. They are but the elements of yesterday's creed which have become incongruous in the setting of to-day. But this is a point to which we shall come back.

Now has the process of Christian history seen a displacement within its own society such as that indicated by a contrast with without? Has religion advanced or receded in the social scale in Europe itself, during the evolution of our modern civilization? The question does not touch the validity of religion, nor its force in individual lives, but is one for history to answer.

First, as to primitive Christianity. Here there is no possibility of doubt. Religion, in the earliest age of the Church, dominated everything. There were miracles and the gift of tongues and the presence of a Holy Spirit revealed in acts of power and visions that drowned out the very horizons of reality. In the age that followed, persecution on the one hand and churchly penance on the other strengthened the fibre and beat together the loose fabric of earlier spiritism. Even in its more rational aspects, the new society fastened upon the religious side of Greek philosophy for a justification of the whole. It could not turn to science for a chastening critique, for there was no science worth turning to. As we said before, the antique world was a distinctly religious one, except where practical affairs had cut through; and Christianity was not a business. So, from whatever angle one takes it, the first chapter of Christian history was one saturated with religion as no subsequent chapter has been. There was little else to saturate it with. We must not forget that Christianity was not all Christian; that it never has been so. It is, and was from the first, drawn from all antiquity, and preserves for us things that were sacred untold ages before there was a temple at Jerusalem. It was a new consecration of consecrated things. However revolutionary it seemed, it kept as much of the old régime as could be applied in the new. The whole process was one of transformation. But the taboos of Christianity gained as much from its victories over those taboos which it rejected as from those which it incorporated into its own doctrines; for the prohibition of sacred things is often the very means for perpetuating the sense of their potency — as things of evil, and the prohibition itself develops into a new taboo. From whatever angle we view it, the world of primitive Christianity was one dominated by religion.

When we turn to the Middle Ages there is still no doubt as to the general character of the situation. Every one admits that the Middle Ages were religious. In fact the tendency is to make them out to be more religious than they really were. They did lack the independent thinkers of antiquity, but they were not without secular triumphs in practical form, in politics and law. Indeed, the national state which they produced was perhaps the first genuine political creation of the secular ideal. The confusion of religion and politics which had marked the city-state was no longer possible when the religion was attached, theoretically at least, to the unworldly city of the soul. The Church, to be sure, did not limit itself to its *patria cœlestis* and presided over as much as it could of mundane things. But the spiritual character of the "Kingdom of Christ" was urged upon forgetful theologians by lawyers and driven home by the men-at-arms in the service of Henry II or Philip IV.

Yet the Middle Ages were religious. Their monuments in the shape of churches and cathedrals are sufficient witness. There is an old and now exploded legend that, as the world approached the year 1000, in penitence and fear of that final date for the coming of Christ it covered itself, as the monkish chronicler said, with the white garment of churches. The legend is false; the creations of that most enduring type of architecture, the Romanesque, were not intended, appropriate as it may seem, to be left here, after the drama of history was over, like sepulchral monuments in the silence of a deserted world. They were built, like those before and after, out of the depth of a religious impulse which had many millenniums instead of one behind it, and passed on with more notable creations still into the centuries that followed. Gothic art is the noblest outward tribute mankind has paid to Christianity. And as religion always confuses itself with other things, the mediæval devotion which it inspired was hallowed by ideals of loveliness. We can have but little idea now of the contrast between the misery of mediæval life and the splendor of the expression of its religion. How magically beautiful the parish church must have been beside the hovels of the serfs who brought it the pathos of their offerings! No other miracle, even of its saints, was more wonderful than this, which transformed the moments spent within its walls to a dream of unearthly peace and kindled the imagination of unimaginative men. Even where culture flourished, in cities and at courts, it merely repeated in loftier form the same contrast with reality and enshrined the same miracles. A flask of oil was responsible for the glory of Rheims Cathedral, the crown of thorns for the Sainte Chapelle.

But we are apt to misinterpret and to exaggerate this mediæval religiosity, to regard it as a thing peculiar to the Middle Ages and to the Christian world. This over-emphasis obscures the real drift of history, since it hides the non-Christian, primitive world which preceded the mediæval, and so gives to what may have been merely a phase of Christianity the appearance of a growth in the religious control of society. There were as many shrines in antiquity as those for mediæval relics. The temples crowned the arx or acropolis as the churches did the cities of Christendom. There were altars at the cross-roads long before the saints appropriated them — altars in the acre plots for the Lares, in the house for the Penates; and the genii were to be propitiated on every hand. Even if we grant such sprites a lessening rôle in the antique world, the real past of the Middle Ages lay in the German forests. Compared with that, mediæval religiosity is not so remarkable. We know strangely little of Teutonic paganism and its scope in society. But we do know that there is not an evidence of the

Church's power, in miracles at its shrines, in awed submission to excommunication, in the stern enforcement of morals, in inquisitions and crusades, that is not to be found in forms less dramatic but probably not less effective throughout the length and breadth of savagery. When the gods of the Teutonic forests yielded before the missionaries of the new religion, it is likely that there was for the time being an accentuation of the rôle of religion in society. But of the subsequent history one cannot be so sure. We have it from the hands of monks and suspect their perspectives. We do know that the age that built the Gothic cathedrals was that in which the lawyers were already building up the king's courts and limiting ecclesiastical jurisprudence. The money which flowed into the church as the tribute to it of society was the very cause of the first assertion of independence on the part of the national state, in the thirteenth century. In fact, the more closely we look into the history of the Middle Ages, the more we see that it was then that the foundations were laid of those political and purely secular structures which were destined to dominate in our own times.

This is not the place, however, to attempt to reconstruct our idea of the Middle Ages, nor to weigh their secular over against their religious elements. For when we turn to modern times we realize that, whatever may have been the secular gains of the Middle Ages, — and they were considerable, — we are now in a different world. A revolution has intervened. We are living in another era, and so vast is the change between our society and that of crusading and cathedral-building Europe that we can hardly realize that the process of that change was already strongly at work so long ago. The secular advance has now so accelerated its pace as to obscure its own past history. We seem as far away from puritan religiosity as from the age of St. Francis and St. Dominic. Yet viewed, not in terms of loss but of gain, that is, in terms of the achievement of secular control, the seventeenth century, with its rise of the merchant class, its national organization for trade and bullion, its rise to power of parliaments, its colonies, literatures, and science, was the very dawn of the new revolutionary era.

Now in the light of all the ages what are

DEVOLUTION OR EVOLUTION? 51

we? Compare our present world not simply with the Middle Ages, but with the Orient, with primitive society and antiquity, and see by contrast what is there that is distinctively ours. We find at once that we, too, share largely in the Oriental, primitive, antique, and mediæval. But we have something more — modernity. And the key to modernity is control. It means that we are facing our problems directly and not in a medium of taboo, that we are working out our destiny with growing self-consciousness and a larger vision of realities.

About the character of that contrast there can be no doubt. It is the same no matter which way we turn. It is a contrast of religious societies against secular. No other society is or has been so secular as ours; nowhere else is the tendency so consistently away from religious control. This is the direction, ostensibly, of what we call our progress. It is the mark of the European as distinguished from the non-European society, of the modern as contrasted with the ancient or mediæval, of the scientific as opposed to the theological.

Examine first the structure of our society. Government is everywhere becoming republican, in reality if not in name. But government was at some time generally, if not universally, the affair of kings. Now kings, real kings, are a product of religion; they are divine or semi-divine, or acquire some fraction of divinity. That is one reason why we republicans, especially in America, cannot understand the attitude toward them of their subjects. They were, in many places, the very incarnation of a god, and where not regarded as divine their persons were, and are, sacred. The rules of court etiquette preserve the spirit of the taboos which they replace. The scepter and diadem, the royal purple — which it was death for a plain Roman citizen to wear, — the apple of empire, thrones and coronation chairs, are substitutes of civilization for those regalia of drums, sticks, and umbrellas, themselves invested with magic power to curse or kill any treasonable person who ventures so much as to touch or even look at them, — such as form the insignia of royalty in Malay. The king alone can handle his regalia. He is himself, like the drum and the umbrella, a thing taboo, a sacred object. His touch, which had been secularized by the seventeenth century to the treatment of skin diseases only, was so charged with " medicine "

DEVOLUTION OR EVOLUTION? 53

in the South Seas that it might kill instead of cure. The divine right of kings and the sacred character of monarchy in general is no fiction of courtly panegyrists, maintained by standing armies. It exists from the dawn of society. Altars to Cæsar may have symbolized the rational forces of law and order, but their meaning for the populations of the empire is not to be sought in the secular activities of any one Cæsar or dynasty of Cæsars, but in that religious awe which still, though in slight degree, George V shares with the kings of the Cannibal Islands.

To-day, however, the divine kingship has disappeared. When, now and again, a Hohenzollern ventures to protest, he is met with a chorus of derision and obliged in future to read speeches prepared for him by his ministers. The regalia in the tower are on public exhibition and injure no profane eyes by their taboo; the king's evil is treated in hospitals. The king himself is a symbol of the past.

Legislation is no longer presided over by those skilled in omens and auguries. Where priests control politics, the judgment of the Western world is that we have a "mediæval" state of affairs. We tend to go so far as to object to them bringing any pressure of religious threat or promise to affect our voters or representatives. Religion still enters into our politics, but only indirectly, through its influence upon each citizen. The basis of religion has shifted from society to the individual. What were the creation and the expression of the group, in which the individual used to share simply because he belonged to the group, has become a matter of personal experience and private judgment. Religion is no longer a thing of the state with us, and is growing less so elsewhere. It is interpreted by the courts of the United States as a personal relationship between God and man,— an idea unthinkable to Roman or Japanese. It does not assume command and dictate action, as it does in Islam and did in ancient Judea. Scruples still to some extent embody the ancient taboo, but they are generally little more than checks upon conduct; seldom are they spurs to positive action, and when they measure their strength with economic interest or national desire for power, they are as weak as Machiavelli believed them to be.

A religion whose scope in public life is reduced to the exhortation of morality is not in

DEVOLUTION OR EVOLUTION? 55

command of the situation. Unless it can interfere and by an act of power compel the allegiance of men, it has lost control. For morality itself is being secularized. We draw the line between sin and crime, and leave sin for punishment in another world. Our police are charged with the public maintenance of our morals, and to touch those morals with emotion gives us but a poor shadow of that religion, which throughout the centuries has surrounded with supernatural terrors every violation of social rule, inflicting with unquestioned power the penalties of disease, mutilation, or death. We see morals now as a problem of our own to work out, not as a cringing to dictates of superstition. Psychology shows us that even our consciences are mainly the echoes of social usages, and so that secret monitor becomes an agent in secularization rather than a clue to divine mysteries. Charity has become a business and a social duty, a thing of the head rather than of the heart, a coöperation in social uplift rather than a mere avenue to saintliness for the giver of alms.

The institutions of the state — those which were once the very nurseries of religion — are the most secular things we have to-day. Law itself was once of divine origin ; now we recognize that it is its very human quality which makes it *law*, as over against taboo on the one hand and morals on the other. The test of law is whether or not it can be enforced by real penalties. Where the sanction is either psychological terror or social disapproval we have no law. Law does not deal so lightly with those who violate it; it does not leave the punishment in the hands of religion or custom. It executes its own judgments, by its own officers. The growth of law is a symbol of the secular state. Compare the English law, for instance, with the Talmud saturated in magic, or with the law of the Mohammedan world, where theology and jurisprudence are indissoluble, and you acquire a new respect for the simple principles of justice which were worked out over questions of Adam the Smith's cabbages or Walter the Miller's cows on the common.

Private property is a mark of civilization. Its protection, now committed to those secular institutions, the courts, was mainly taken over by them from religion. Although violence and the law of might share with religion the credit of originating and perpetuating personal possession, taboo (the luck or curse in things themselves) is the most powerful sanction primitive society knows. It is so strong as to resist secularization — into civil law — except where secularization is most vigorous. Even the life of secular Europe runs along within the grooves of custom based on taboo, much more than within the formal stipulations of law. In Polynesia, where taboo is strongest, the civil law has hardly got a start. The system of taboo is itself sufficient. There a wisp of grass tied to an object is enough to make it one's own, by arming it with the terrors of religion. Possession is nowhere more readily recognized than where the belief in contagious magic prevails. The stone that you have fashioned acquires a part of you. Break it, you suffer. Steal it, the owner is within your power. The beads you wear become you; if they are charmed beads they will not let another touch them without hurting him. They will burn his hand, or bring him bad luck. One need not go to Polynesia for such ideas. They are familiar to us from childhood. The idea of personal property is not a creation of the civil law, but the law a creation of it.

Politics and religion are now seldom linked by us except by way of contrast. This may be partly due to that theology which reaches back to beyond Augustine and opposes the Church to the World. But the opposition is taken up now from the other side; politics insists upon it most. The politician who handles his politics according to the precepts of his religion is marked out either for fame or ridicule — perhaps for both. Fame awaits the success in such difficult emprise, but ridicule is sure to come if there is not behind the judgments which he forms a strong, good sense which does not allow the religion to go too far. If his spiritual guidance is likely to lead to economic ruin, it is rejected as out of place. Madero's spiritistic inspirations, for instance, were the main source of his undoing. So, as society organizes itself more and more efficiently, it places the burden of its control in hands directly responsible to it. The statesman who is too religious may come to regard himself as a belated successor of the king by divine right, responsible to God alone. However noble his aspiration, society is suspicious of such a man, unless he proves his worth by success in worldly things. It labels him a visionary, and invites to its councils practical men who know what they and society need here and now. No voices in dreams disturb the Hannibals or Constantines of to-day; and, as superstition ceases its direct interference, orthodoxy accommodates itself to a less dominant rôle. Men fall back upon themselves. Forced to work out their own destiny by deliberate choice, they strengthen and perfect the organs of social judgment. Constitution-making in our modern states is a war upon arbitrary action. It limits more and more the scope of emotional impulses. It safeguards the achievements of the age-long struggle for control.

Just as the structure of modern society is less religious than that of those which lack modernity, so is custom, that unwritten constitution of the commonplace, that mirror of social habit and outlook. Custom is the reservoir of conservatism, and it perpetuates most of our old taboos. It prescribes the whole régime of what is "good form." Yet even in this sphere the secular processes are at work. Take our holidays, for instance. They do not have much to do with religion now. They are seldom "holy days." The saints — as such — have disappeared from all ordinary calendars, along with the gods who preceded them and in whose honor the calendar itself was invented. St. Patrick furnishes the occasion for a procession on Fifth Avenue. St. George is honored by a dinner. But the birthday of George Washington or Queen Victoria or the anniversary of the taking of the Bastille share equal honors with even national saints' days. It is only when one reads deeply into ancient history and sees how time itself was first marked out by sacred barriers, or when one sees the fearful power of the primitive periods of taboo, that one realizes where we have got in our secularization of time.

There is growing up a new morality, which substitutes for the old beliefs a sense of human needs; a new morality to which religion accommodates itself. The Church emphasizes more and more its non-religious aspects, its secular appeal, its ideal leadership in the brotherhood of man. Young Men's Christian Associations advertise their swimming-baths. They boast a culture of the body like Greek pagans instead of ascetic virtues of Christian saints, and sometimes try to make religion attractive by placing the accent on other things. Yet in spite of such efforts, church-going, if gaining at all, is by no means keeping pace with the gain in its worldly rivals. The week-end excursion is a modern invention. Cathedrals in France are maintained as national monuments of art. Charles Booth has shown in his great survey of London that only about one quarter of the people in that city of churches ever see the inside of one. Cinematographs and paid singers fail to hold the working-class. And this is in a sphere where custom — and taboo — counts most. To be sure, many facts may be cited against these; religious activity cannot be measured easily in statistics. But we are not dealing here with the question of whether people are more or less religious than they used to be, but whether they make religion more or less an element in society. We must look at the total trend of custom, as of institutional development, not merely at isolated examples.

Now there is no larger social fact in the modern world than its national free education. Such a force for moulding the ideas of the coming generations was never in the control of secular powers in any previous age. Religion has realized the importance of it, and only where warring creeds refuse to compromise has the Church acquiesced in the existence of such an agent of unreligion. But the secular schools, although they have to fight for their existence, — and they seem face to face with serious attacks in America, — have become an ideal of democracy, whose militant forces in Europe at the polls face anathemas undaunted to secure for the children an education in which science and enlightenment shall be untouched by dogma. There is the same trend in the curricula of colleges and universities. Theological faculties dwarf or disappear. Theological presidents grow fewer and fewer, while twenty years ago they were in control almost everywhere. Even the great public schools of England, where mellowing tradition lasts so long, have begun to fall into the hands of laymen. A clerical school law passed last year in Belgium brought the country to the verge of revolution. France is committed irrevocably to the secular school system, and the Sorbonne, that greatest centre of scholastic theology, is entirely in the hands of the anti-clerical. In Germany the battle is still on, but the majority of the nation has definitely pronounced for secularization. The present generation is determined that the next shall meet its problems untrammeled by theological presuppositions.

The outlook of humanity is changing even more than its institutions or its customs. These will follow the outlook. The meaning of it all is to be found in the work of science. We must not forget that science is but a few years old. There was none ever — none worth talking of — before our time. It is already the largest influence, the most vital force in the world to-day. It does not enter the field of emotion, in which most of our lives are passed, and console or cheer us with the promise of immortality, but it places power in the hands of intelligence, and makes devotee and skeptic alike work at its machines, build its cities and prepare its laboratories. It is not merely the subtle thought secreted in a brain, but it is incorporated in iron and steel and moves in the forces of nature. It has remade the universe, and restated the mystery thereof in its own terms.

The wind does not now blow where it listeth, but where other things — heat and pressures — list that it shall blow. Disease is no longer a divine affliction, but a violation or consequence of natural laws. The battle between science and the old religion has been a real one, and the result in any case is not the defeat of science. In so far as control of society is concerned, Dr. Osler is justified in saying of religion that "The battle of Armageddon has been fought — and lost."

We might carry the evidence of this secularizing trend of the modern world through every department of intellect or action. Philosophy gives up its absolutes and interprets phenomena in terms of evolution. History, in form as well as content, mirrors the change, as the myths of the gods give way to the epic of the hero, and then, through lessening miracles, the chronicle, born in the temple and nourished in the monastery, becomes at last the purely human story of purely human things. Even language reflects the process in its colorless words. "Psychology," for instance, brings up no image of the maiden Psyche, or the breath of life which also became "spirit." Just as our bodies are museums of comparative anatomy, with traces of every ancestor from the first cell-protoplasm up, so in our society we retain the religious organs of the past. But like the muscles of a claw which are obliged to hold this pencil with which I write, they are more and more subordinated to other things.

Augustine's dream of the City of God has not been realized. The City of Satan — of primitive and primal religious belief — was stronger than he dreamed. But the great City of Religion, whose walls include the seven seas, and which has held within them the aspirations and fears of untold centuries, is now giving way to the City of Man. And the new city is a *civitas terrena;* it gives up ideals that suited a world to come for practical politics in a stern present. Its characteristic monuments are not temples or cathedrals. It has a place for them alongside its libraries, colleges, and hospitals; but they are only one symbol of its aspiration. It is less interested in heaven and hell than in unemployment and sanitation. It is cleaning streets and tearing down our slums. If religion blocks the way of its reforms, it labels that religion superstition and brushes it from its path. Even its evils are frankly human; its lust for power, its rivalries, wars and armaments, the slavery it owns in factory and mine, the idleness and luxury its industry produces. We have no illusions about these things. They are ours, for better or worse. We are responsible for them, and know it. We can no longer escape by claiming that its good or ill are God's or Satan's. The City of Civilization is in our hands; and the knowledge that it rests with us to make it fit to be the symbol of either is the inspiration to make it worthy the dignity of man.

Eppur si muove! It is now the turn of the theologian to repeat the muttered phrase of Galileo. And with equal justice. Religion moves, vast and potent, in the world to-day. One must be blind, indeed, not to see the evidences of its power in both the structure and the movement of our modern world. Indeed, when we turn from the external contrasts of history and anthropology to the question of its vitality we strike a different problem. Religion seems as constant a factor in humanity as gravitation in the material world. But whereas gravitation is most in evidence where there is motion, and eludes detection where things are at rest,— although rest, being a counterpoise of forces, really embodies more motion,— religion, on the other hand, is most in evidence where society is standing still, in the slowly moving East or the still more static savagery. In the swift movement of modern life it may hide itself as gravitation does in the immutable.

We are pressing our metaphor like an inquisitor; but it is time we opened the inquisition upon this proposition of the secular advance, which has kept us occupied so long. For, the moment we lose sight of the non-Christian world, and give up our external measurement, the perspective, which seemed so straight when viewed from central Australia or Rangoon, becomes a labyrinth. We are at once confronted with a mass of contradictions. The outlines of history and the tendencies of to-day become obscured. The growth of social control, which, viewed from without, seems to mark modern effort, is dragged like a vanquished thing in the wake of incalculable forces, apparently ignorant even of its existence. The evolution of our secular civilization, when examined more closely, seems hardly more than a slight rearrangement of the elements in previous stages of society. The world to-day is surely but a mere readjustment to new conditions of essentially the same things as made up the world of the savage. *Plus ça change, plus ça reste la même chose!*

The modern world is, after all, very primitive — and very religious. Religion is identified, by us, as by all other people, with established order and upright conduct; it is a bulwark of conservatism and a slogan for reform. The structure of our society shows this at a glance. We do not demand that our politicians shall be religious men, but we do demand that they should not be irreligious, — frankly and actively opposed to our religion. Religion may not now interfere as it used to with the policies of state, but it forces from those hostile or indifferent the tribute of silence or hypocrisy. What Voltaire called the "infamous thing" turns the brand of infamy upon those who would so brand it. The very name of Voltaire, whom a great theologian recently termed the greatest religious leader of modern times, is still execrated by the society whose sense he outraged by too revolutionary methods of reform. "Atheist" and "infidel" are names of ignominy, even when the victim stands among the intellectual leaders of the race; because unbelief is social sacrilege. If committed in public it marks a man out for the aversion of society — not merely of the Church, but of common, everyday society — as it does in the primitive world. Such anarchists of religion are likely to find themselves excluded from that great fraternity of mutual trust and friendly confidence which holds the rights of citizenship in the City of the Respectable. To be sure, the ban of society is not so effective as in primitive life or in the Middle Ages. The modern culprit is not so likely to suffer from the psychological terrors of the taboo, and the effective engines of conformity are lacking. With him it is only a question of morals, inducing, not enforcing, compliance. But the attitudes are much the same.

When we turn from public to private life, religion is stronger yet, for the religion of the West is mainly personal. The amount varies, to be sure, for in the modern world, where independent judgment plays some rôle, even when one finds uniformity in action there is by no means bound to be uniformity in belief. Conformity in action tends to bring conformity in creed, as we see in the Catholic sons of converted Huguenots in France and elsewhere; but when faith is open to all the influences of science, business, politics, and industry, as it is with us, and each of these plays in upon the other, distracting interest and commanding attention, the amount of vitality of any one factor, and of religious belief in particular, not only varies between every two individuals, but varies in the individual so that it is never the same at any two moments. Up and down our streets there is as much variation in our fellow-citizens in superstition, religion, mysticism, and their opposites, as in the property they own, the work they do, or the clothes they wear. But in spite of variations, religion, little or much, is a common denominator of the mental outlook of the vast mass of modern citizenship, just as property is the common mark of their respectability.

The strength of religion is threefold, in habits, both of body and mind, in conscious belief, from superstition to reasoned creeds, and in mysticism. These interwork, and in modern religion all three are generally present. Of them, habit is the strongest, and mysticism the weakest, while faith serves as a sort of bridge between the two, reaching from the dimmest flicker of appreciation of habitual acts to the bold conceptions of scholastic theology, from perceived sensations to reasoned systems of the universe.

Habit is the thing that holds the world together, civilized as well as uncivilized. It is the largest thing in society as it is in individual life. There it is embodied in institutions, laws, and morals; here in action, acquiescence, routine. Originality, the rejection of habit, is a rare gift; at least it is exhibited in small quantities. Society accepts it as a pleasant diversion so long as the exhibition is not to be taken too seriously; but, when originality shows its true anarchic colors, a very slight amount of it is all that is needed to send one to prison or the asylum, as it once brought outlawry and lynching. It is a denial of the infallibility of the commonplace; and through the evolution of our species, from the horde of gregarious animals, that kill their abnormal members, to the inquisition and to the immigration laws of the United States, no penalty has been surer than that of extermination or exclusion for it. So habit and custom rule. Few people are either shockingly original or care to be thought so, and what happens to those who are is a lesson to the rest of us. Moreover the habits and customs we follow are, in the main, of untold antiquity. Just as they are not only not our own, but other people's, they are not simply of our time, but of all the past. They are the largest records of human history. Their vitality does not depend upon consciousness; habits are stronger than thought. They exemplify a sort of perpetual motion. Once started they can keep going, until interrupted by others, long after their original impulse is lost, because each generation which repeats them furnishes a further impulse toward their perpetuation.

Now, since habit is largely the persistence of the primitive, and the primitive was and is so largely religious, the religious habits and customs of to-day have a strength which it is impossible to measure. As a matter of fact, religion is so much a thing of habit that it has escaped analysis until our own time, and has been taken for granted as an essential element in society. There was no problem of religion as such until the eighteenth century. It hardly exists yet for the mass of our fellow-citizens. We are apt to forget this, those of us who get within the problem. But most of the people with whom we live take religion as much as a matter of course as they take their meals.

How much of a vision of secularization does one get from viewing the capitalistic agents of the secular advance seated in upholstered pews, the workers crowding to morning mass, the forces of production stilled one seventh of the time at the behest of religion? Churchgoing may be falling off, but still, as in Goethe's boyhood, the church-bell goes out into the fields and hunts the truants, and it gathers them in wherever its note of authority falls on the willing ear of habit. Some escape; but the significant thing is that even the indifferent are generally ready to apologize for their indifference and acknowledge their guilt. Society puts its brand upon nonconformity, and demands that religion at least shall be treated — as religion ought to be!

There are habits of thought as well as of action. Thought is perhaps too limited a word, for the mental processes which are dominated by habit stretch back to the beginning. But after thought awakens, it is mostly busy as the advocate of habit. It is still the apologist for most of what we do, rather than the directing cause. We feel that this or that is right; a subtle intimation guides us in our choice. We call it conscience; it is just crystallized habit. For our consciences are less our own than other people's. Conscience is the intrusion of society into our own affairs. The inner light to which the Quaker turns as to the inspiration of God is in reality the deepest voice of religion, for it is the concentrated essence of the primitive, moulded by taboo, tested by untold centuries of social experience and speaking with the authority of the unanalyzed. The mind can hold this reflex of primitive attitudes in almost unlimited quantities. One can see its variations in people, like the trembling needle that registers the electricity in the dynamo. The electricity is the force of tradition and society; the conscience is merely the indicator of its presence.

It is habit, too, which is the main element in that sort of sixth sense which a group of obscurantist psychologists have been of late trying to foist upon society, — that subliminal or periphery or whatever it may be. There is no more a religious sense than an economic or business sense. The subliminal is merely the subconscious; and the subconscious is mainly accumulated habit. Although it is based on more than our own experience, it does not register more than the remains of that great experience of the society, past as well as present, out of which we have sprung. Its thrills are never, at their best, more than the perpetuation of habitual reactions acquired somewhere, somehow in the long schooling of humanity, and transmitted, like the nerves in which they reside, from our ancestors. The sensations of subliminal religion are as near as we can get to an animal's appreciation of phenomena. The habit goes back that far.

Next to habit in religion, comes faith, habit's more or less conscious apologist. Habit itself is not all it seems to be. It is often very misleading. It is the receptacle, in which much of our religion is preserved, but one cannot tell by looking at the outside how much there is really contained within. The man who takes his religion as he takes his meals, or wears it as he does his clothes, may have very little of it in what he calls his heart. Even the subliminal religion of a perplexed philosopher is less religious than he supposes. It is not until these habitual reactions pass into the realm of consciousness and become faith that we can appreciate their vitality. Faith is the element of our religion upon which we place most emphasis — simply because it is the conscious element. Its scope is enormous. It connects, on the one hand, with those dumb attitudes which are bred of habit in the nervous organisms of animals and on the other with the most profound conceptions of the human intellect. Taken historically it is hardly more than the science of habit, the explanation, in terms of current thought, of actions and attitudes, so fastened upon us as to seem instinctive. But since it explains things in terms of themselves, grants legitimacy to what is, apologizes for thrills by insisting on the mystery, it is the largest agent of conservatism in the world, and the most potent source of religious vitality.

No one can measure the extent of faith in the modern world. Few of us know how much we have ourselves. But if a man from Mars were to visit our rational Europe, he would undoubtedly find, as the most remarkable anomaly of our civilization, as Professor Pratt has so graphically depicted it,[1] our practically universal belief in the existence of a God whom none of us has ever seen, in his justice in the face of the tragedy of helpless innocence

[1] Cf. J. B. Pratt, *The Psychology of Religious Belief*, pp. 3–5.

which makes up the scheme of evolution, in his goodness in spite of the sufferings of men for others' sins, in his omnipotence, although the laws of the universe seem to admit of no interfering hand. We are so accustomed to this faith, it comprises so much of our worldview, that we forget how much it really dominates our intellects.

Alongside of this fundamental belief, there is a world of others. Mythology is perhaps the first expression of reason. The child and the savage see things as a mere succession of events. It is always "and then another thing happened." Description is narrative; cause and result are the beginning and end of a story. The mythological faculty is the basis of more in our philosophy than we dream of. It has drawn what Huxley called the veil of Isis over the phenomena of this world. We have the same tendency to believe the presuppositions of the myth as to accept the myth itself. The critical faculty is a late acquisition; belief is much more natural. There is everything in its favor. It is social, — an acquiescence in what society declares, — while criticism is individual and involves independence, not simply of judgment but of standpoint. We all tend to believe; to disbelieve generally demands more effort than most people devote to a problem.

The strength of faith, in credulity on the one hand and thoughtful acceptance of creed on the other, is impossible of measurement. But one can see the evidences of its vitality outside as well as inside orthodoxy. Even in the heart of rationalism one can see the same persistence of — let us call it — credulity as in the cultured circles of antiquity. Where Christianity has lost its appeal, Asiatic cults come in, as they did in pagan Rome when Christianity was one of them. Where time-worn ideals of orthodoxy fail to convince, we have phenomena like those of Christian Science. Buddhism is gaining, so I am told, even among German university professors! The fact that those who are at work in social service, even in the cause of the secular advance, find an emotional satisfaction in viewing their work as religion, apart from creeds and on a purely human ground, and the pathetic eagerness with which the awakening consciousness of a newly educated democracy turns this way and that for religious leadership, are crowning tributes to the hold it has upon us in the modern world — even when we seem to be slipping away from its immemorial claims.

Here comes the rôle of mysticism — modern mysticism, that is. It attempts to be both critical and believing. It sees the veil of Isis torn by science, but regards the veil itself as a phenomenon as real as those phenomena which it conceals. Its roots are in the same tendencies as are in habit and dogma; but it is aware of the need for adjustment. It is a sort of belief in belief itself; a criticism which starts with acceptance and therefore ends with it. It is the rationalizing of an unrational — though not necessarily irrational — tendency. But the tendency is older than consciousness, as deep as life, and as universal as the tragic history of society. Mysticism is the orthodoxy of heresies, the sanction of individual religion by the faculties and the judgments which have produced society. But being individual, it is hard to estimate — harder than faith of the orthodox type because it lives under various disguises. All we can do here is to call attention to its rôle in the perplexed world of to-day, and to note how, through it, religion invades the most positive creations of science and registers the limitations of the intellect. Its field, moreover, passes the boundaries of faith, and includes, rightly or wrongly, the highest aspirations of those moral leaders in the secular world, who see poetry in justice and beauty in the moral order of the universe, and fuse will and imagination into the emotional apprehension of those forces which make for righteousness.

The conclusion is commonplace. Religion plays a part in modern life the scope of which we ordinarily are hardly aware of, simply because it is so much a matter of course. It still presides over the crises of most men's lives, as it does in the Australian wilderness. Life may largely escape its control in the affairs of business and demands of duty or pleasure; but, in the face of death and in times of suffering and bereavement, in those tragic hours when the bewildered emotions beat vainly at the blank walls of thought, religion resumes its reign over the mass of humanity. It rises shining from the dust and dullness of habit and gives meaning to ceremonies and strength to outworn beliefs. Superstition, orthodoxy, and mysticism all respond to life's alarms. Its helplessness is their strength. Behind all, the sense of the impending doom — the uncertainty of everything except that the doom is sure — lends to religion, to all appearances, the inevitability of death itself.

And yet the religious revolution is a fact. It is a fact which does not rest upon any weak assertion of mine. It is asserted by the very structure of society, by the current of its thought and the push of its tremendous movement, by the creations of that scientific spirit which is now stretching out the control of our bodies to conquer the forces of nature and of our minds to grasp its hidden problems. And back of the religious revolution lies the tremendous process of social evolution, of emancipation from superstition and the awakening of reason. Society, as I said before, is "carving out for itself, from the realm of mystery in which it lies, a sphere of unhampered action and a field of independent thought."

What is the significance of such vast contradictions and parallels? This will be the subject of our later lectures.

III

THE PROBLEM AND THE DATA

ON the basis of a large comparison of modern civilization with Oriental, primitive, and antique, we risked the statement, which, if true, is one of the most tremendous facts in the history of mankind — that the progress of civilization has been also a process of secularization. Then we looked for objections to this hypothesis, and saw, even in a hurried survey of the vitality of modern religious movements, reasons for hesitancy in accepting it.

The impressive strength of these movements and the apparent inevitability of the religious outlook in the face of mysteries, persistent and insoluble, seem in themselves sufficient answer to the claim that religion is a lessening social force. And yet, in the new horizons of anthropology and history, no clearer perspective stretches out before us than that which leads from our secular and rational civilization to the magic and superstition of primitive men. The revolutionary movement of science in our own day, which no one questions, takes its place as part of a long historical process, and is apparently as inevitable, in its turn, as the mysteries which it brushes aside. For if mystery lies in the very situation of life, where intelligence is forever facing things un-understood, skepticism lies in the very nature of intelligence.

But another objection to our proposition remains to be considered, this time a criticism of method rather than of results. Our scheme of evolution was the result of contrast between ourselves and the non-European. If one looks for contrasts, one accentuates the points of difference; but what if we should look for resemblances instead? The moment we do, we find them almost as impressive and convincing as the differences.

Take the Orient. If the West lack its religious institutions, and has but little use for idle Yogis, sunning themselves on the steps of its busy temples or by its broad roads of commerce, that is not to say that it lacks religion. All that one can say, until one has studied the situation deeply, is that it lacks the Yogis. We have given up the rigidity of the East, and the more complex and mobile character of Western life reduces religion to subtler forms.

But the contrast may be one of form rather than of content.

Similarly, the savage, who seems to us so dominated by taboo, may be, and likely is, much more religious to us than to himself, — especially if we are hunting for his religion. Taboos, like civilized etiquette, may stand athwart conduct without one knowing that they are really there. It is only when one breaks them, or runs upon them unaware, that one realizes their explosive power. The savage, with less introspection, is less conscious of the religion in these mysterious things than the investigators who trace the relationships. His life, narrowly limited at best, fits all the more easily its scheme of routine and inherited belief. And in most things he acts about as we do.

We meet the same paradox when we turn to our own history. There is another side to it as well as that vision of secularization which we saw in it, in the last lecture. Is not the rationalist stretching a theory to the limit if he makes the evolution of civilization a vast and steady process of secular advance and a narrowing of the social sphere of religion, when most of the great epochs of that history show its power? Christianity itself, for instance, is probably the largest single phenomenon of European history. There is little spectacle of secularization in the way it rose on the very ruins of antiquity to furnish guidance and ideals for the youth of this civilization of to-day. It assumed control of barbarian states, and, in the long upward struggle of succeeding centuries, its organization was the one common embodiment of social gain, the asylum for learning and the museum for art. The moral empire of the mediæval Church has no parallel in history, with its undisputed sway over the minds and consciences of men, with its priesthood " panoplied with inviolability " and armed with the powers of eternal life and death in sacrament and excommunication. Religion is no dead thing inside the structure of a church, whose very persistence rests upon the unbroken habits and continued faith of humanity. Without that faith, shared by society at large, excommunication would lose its terrors, inquisitions and censorships be unheeded, sacrament and priestly control be impossible. And time after time that vitality has shown itself. Reformations and religious revivals mark some of the largest epochs of Europe, and from them radiate influences of incalculable scope. Think of the movements they inaugurated: monks of Cluny starting a reform that swept the Papacy from the control of factions of murderous Roman nobles to the headship of a regenerated Church and a power more imperial than that of the Empire; recluses of Clairvaux drawing the ideals of an iron age to thoughts of peace or bursting forth with the message of crusade; Franciscans and Dominicans penetrating the first slums of the new commercial cities, and defying the sordid march of wealth with the poetic dream of apostolic poverty; Lutherans and Calvinists furnishing the moral courage to the individual for the attainment of a Christian liberty — under theological tutelage; Puritans whose sober common sense transplanted that idea of liberty into the secular world, — but whose stern and rigid faith remained, like the shadow of a great cathedral, darkening the bright city of the world they scorned but fought for; the molten enthusiasm of modern evangelicalism gathering its force in movements like that of Methodism which swept the secular complacency of the eighteenth century in England like a river of fire. These things stand out on the path of European history, and no interpretation in terms of economics or stressing of other perspectives can get rid of them. They reveal the vital impulses of men; and no one knows how much of such dormant energy there is among us to-day.

The history of Europe seems little enough like a chronicle of secularization when one looks over the achievements of Christianity. The same is true of its neighbor and rival Islam. Its history is even more to the point; for whereas Christianity was slow to win recognition and took four centuries to achieve the mastery of the Roman state, Mohammedanism came like a thing inspired, a veritable breath of God, and in a single lifetime galvanized the unsuspected forces of Arabia, which had lain there for untold ages, into a power for world-conquest, — a power that is still conquering.

Both history and anthropology seem to contradict themselves. Looking one way down the perspectives of social evolution we see the narrowing sphere of religion; looking another way we see its persistent and potent interference. And the Orient and savagery reveal similarities apparently as convincing as their contrasts. That contrast between primitive societies dominated by religion and a modern civilization characterized by secular ideals and activities, which underlies our main hypothesis, seems to be growing more and more obscure. Some of us must have already confirmed our intuitive suspicion that it is both superficial and misleading. Similarities do not at first attract attention like differences, but when once we are aware of them they seem more fundamental. The traveler is first struck with the external differences in custom and speech which give a tone to the countries he visits; but after long residence he discerns how under these outer marks of so varied impression are concealed the aspirations and outlook of a common humanity. So he comes later to ignore the differences as at first he ignored the similarities. The one may be as much exaggeration as the other; but he feels, with much justice, that of the two, the recognition of the identities rests generally on the deeper knowledge.

As a matter of fact, these objections leave our proposition quite untouched. It goes without saying that there is an essential likeness in all societies. But one cannot get rid of the comparative and historical survey by merely hiding it behind an accumulated mass of similarities. Contrasts are not less significant than likenesses; indeed their detection forms the first step in criticism, enabling us to classify our distinctions in categories of knowledge. The only problem, after all, is to distinguish the apparent from the real. The scientific mind recognizes that the very contrasts of phenomena arise out of a common base, otherwise the phenomena would not admit of comparison; but it moves to the unifying synthesis through an analysis of distinguishable data. Thus Darwin developed the essential unity of life by a study of the variations of species.

If, however, we accept the contention which we have just been considering, that religion occupies a practically constant place in varying cultures, it argues for, rather than against our hypothesis. We have not maintained that religion is growing less, but that it is less in relation to other things. The difference is in them rather than in it. Religion is our heritage; art and science are our achievements. Grant that the religious heritage has changed, that we have remade it and pass it on improved and purified, it still reflects attitudes older than all civilization. The essential difference between ourselves and the un-modern world lies less in it than in those creations of the human intellect which are distinctly ours, those which make for knowledge and power. Civilization connotes property, intelligence, emancipation — social and individual — and rational control. In these things of the secular spirit lies the vital contrast with the uncivilized, and not in a constant factor like religion, except in so far as it changes to fit the new environment.

When we attempt, however, to reduce our hypothesis to more definite terms, we see why so varying opinions exist concerning it. For no careful, detailed examination of the data has yet been made. So far we have been merely amusing ourselves with impressions, and such impressionistic glimpses as have been given throw but little light upon any solution. In the vast horizons of both East and West, it is possible to arrange contrasts and similarities much as one wishes, just as history so easily, and perhaps inevitably, responds to the bent of the historian, because it contains enough varied material to suit many different perspectives. In the wealth of detail of either past or present one may find material to prove almost any theory. We must get down to more rigid methods.

But now we come to the crux of the situation: the scientific apparatus for its solution is lacking. There has been no serious attempt — in any large way — to face the problem. The group of religious sciences, on the one hand, and that of social sciences, on the other, seldom have any real inter-relations. The reason for this is clear. The social sciences are intruders, or at best prosperous rivals, cultivating soil which once could have produced theologies. So while the old dogmatic studies have resented their intrusion, and now and again burned their treatises in the marketplace, the new sciences on their part have mainly been glad to leave religion as much alone as they could, and so fasten their eyes upon the new structure of which they are the architects and guardians, rather than upon that which they have left. The only serious attention which the problem — or hypothesis — of secularization has aroused is on the part of religion. But apart from sporadic efforts of individual workers, gathering statistical data, little has been done that is not openly apologetic. This is perhaps inevitable. But the blindness of the social sciences — for which they are hardly to blame historically — is no credit to them now, and the greatest single impediment to a proper understanding of that society with whose impulses and habits they attempt to deal. The weakness lies in their unhistorical and unpsychological habit of mind. Bred in the air of the national state, and intent upon problems of secular control, they have failed to see how the monarchies for which they work, the liberties which they expound, the propriety which they safeguard, the homes they protect, the morals whose sanctions they invoke, the justice whose ideals lead them on, are derived from or rooted in religion, and in some cases wear still the shackles of irrational taboos even in the heart of critical skepticism. The social sciences have left religion to theology. They might as well leave finance to bankers or war to soldiers. To be sure, their silence has been, and possibly still is, a discreet one, a tacit recognition of the power of religion rather than a failure to recognize its strength. Its anathemas still reach into laboratory and library, and the secular sciences need not invite more troubles than they have at present. But the result has been to leave the largest factor in social evolution almost unnoticed by the sciences which are supposed to analyze society.

This will be the case until social psychology is admitted alongside economics and history. The objection may very well be raised that social psychology has to come into existence before it can attain recognition. But it cannot get beyond a few rude principles until it enters the fellowship of the social group; and sociology will remain weak and unrespected until it feeds its young psychological ally with statistics and clothes it liberally with the varied garments of phenomena. Until psychology enters the social laboratory, not simply as a chance visitor, but as a worker with chair and deskroom, we shall be groping over our most fundamental problems, and our syntheses of social movements — past or present — will continue to be the guesses they have been. They will continue to be mere guesses at best for a long time to come, but it is something to appreciate the importance of the other element in a guess, the part that does not happen! The potential is a fact as well as the actual. It appears in actualities to some degree, in limitations upon impulse, thought, or action, and in interference of scope or direction. But if what does happen baffles measurement in our complex society, even with the best of instruments at our disposal, how are we to measure what does not happen? Yet something must be done with it, or we do not really know what actually takes place! Indeed, one might claim that to neglect potentialities is to neglect the largest element in life, since after all so little happens compared with the forces which are at work to produce the result.

It is mainly in this region that our problem falls. No one knows what crises or opportunity will bring out of one, nor what latent depths of primeval stuff one covers with the mask of conformity. Still less can society gauge its capacities or limitations. Circumstance seems to stand athwart history like old Fortuna, a goddess of a wayward bent, and more or less a cousin of the Fates. The social sciences are never sure of her caprice. She finds as much capacity for Metternich reactions as for French Revolutions, for clerical obscurantism as for the doctrine of the Rights of Man. No one knows how the most indifferent and blasé societies may yield before a new

Wesley or Savonarola. In the midst of the era of Darwin and physical science, when the intellect had seemed to justify itself by the most triumphant of its creations, come the onslaught of Bergsonian anti-rationalism and the mysticism of James, and the philosophic schools flock to them, as they used to pitch their tents around Abélard on the slopes of Mont-Sainte-Geneviève.

Some potentialities can be measured by experiment, as steam in the steam engine. But the experiments of society can never be exactly repeated, since new factors enter into them every moment. Yet we can arrive at a fair theory of probabilities if we have long observation and careful registering of phenomena; and if social psychology can achieve instruments for accurate measurement of responses to stimuli, it, too, may some day become a science. So far the science of statistics has not ventured into the realm of taboo, but huddles up timidly and diffidently beside the science of economics. Until there is a statistical measurement of religious phenomena, extending over a long enough period of history to enable the anomalous to be disposed of and the normal past to be compared with the normal present, we shall not be able to establish with certainty the interpretations of the problem before us. For actual changes are almost as hard to gauge as unrealized potentialities. Change does not take place in the full light of consciousness. It takes place in two stages of consciousness, the past and the present; and by the time we have changed we cease to realize what we were. Changes in feeling are especially intangible; feeling generally comes and slips away unnoticed. Who of us can say just when we cease to mourn in bereavements or to respond to the myths of childhood? The emotions pass and blend like tones of music, but no one knows just when their echoes die.

Now it has been clear from the start that everything depends upon what we mean by religion. And few of us know. We seldom face the subject as a whole. We limit ourselves to our own variety, and mark it off by arbitrary barriers, calling some forms magic, others superstition, and placing mythology and folk-lore partly outside, partly within. In this way religion as a whole eludes definition. Indeed, many scientific investigators,

THE PROBLEM AND THE DATA

following the example of William James, are now inclined to give up defining it altogether. For this man's religion is not that man's, nor that age's the religion of this; yet the one religion is just as genuine as the other. No single definition can be at the same time all-comprehensive and fit all the varieties. Besides, if one could find such a definition it would be quite useless; for, including everything, it would lend significance to nothing in particular. What we want is not a statement of every element which every one wants included in religion, but a sorting-out of the elements to see if there are any in common, any which therefore seem fundamental in the whole complex. Those common elements never make up the whole of any one variety of religion, in the very nature of the case. But in them, if one should be able to find them, one has a clue to the evolution of the whole group.

This process seems simple. Yet it is not so easy to follow as one might suppose, for our habits of thought are all set another way. There are two possible ways of looking at religion, — one historical, the other we may call contemporary. The historical is a view of it as a process, begun in the dawn of society and still under way; the unhistorical is based upon what goes under the name of religion to-day or at any given time. The one is dynamic, the other static. The historical reaches back along the line of evolution; while the unhistorical reaches out into the world of everyday. The historical view must include the essentials in the religion of an African savage, a Hindoo Brahman, or a Christian; the contemporary need concern itself only with the particular one of these which we happen to be. It is obvious, therefore, that when we speak of a displacement of religion in society, we are referring to the historical conception and not to the contemporary, for only the historical has an evolution. Yet the contemporary, lacking the limitations of history, is likely to seem the universal and absolute, and we shall have to be constantly upon our guard against it, especially since it corresponds more definitely with our experience.

A moment's thought upon the subject shows that these two cannot be the same, since evolution means change and therefore implies that each contemporary religion differs in some way from each past. Yet we

never seem to give it that moment's thought.
We are so thoroughly unhistorical in our habits of mind that it never occurs to us to conceive religion as a process, any more than the Constitution of the United States as a flux. Yet if we could apply enough imagination to our constitutional law, we might even see that stately embodiment of our national aspiration moving with the potent forces of the people's will. Through crisis and amendment it broadens out, clumsily adapting itself to circumstance. For it, like every other institution of society, is not a thing existing by itself, but a living organism, sharing the life of the society whose aims it embodies. So with religion. Viewed historically, it is not merely a series of contemporary religions, but an embodiment of continuous if changing elements. It changes with them, but is more than any one phase. It penetrates varying forms as the life of the nation does the Constitution. In short, history is more than a register of separate series, a putting-together of successive but disassociated facts. Our problem, in dealing with the history of religion, is therefore one in dynamics, a weighing of moving forces, not a measurement of data at rest.

Religion in the historical sense is not any one religion of any one time, but the element which is constant throughout the whole process. Of course, as we said above, that leaves it less than any one religion. The common denominator gives no clue to the number or size of the things it may enter into. For instance, to go back to our old arithmetics, 2 is the common denominator of 6 and 10 and 26, but it furnishes no suggestion of the other factors, 3, 5, or 13. In terms of this figure of speech, the modern religions might be said to be composed of a vast number of thirteens, the antique a great number of fives, and even the primitive to have quite an assortment of threes. The common denominator is less than all the other factors. So, the common element in religion is perhaps less in evidence in some religions than many other elements peculiar to them.

Now, what is the value of a common denominator — or definition — in terms so low? There would be little, indeed, if our problem were really one in mathematics. But we have been pushing our figure too far. For the data with which we have to deal are those of life, where analyses of mathematics do not hold. The data of life do not arrange themselves like integers alongside one another. They fuse and blend. The elements of religion, as I said before, are in constant flux, and a common denominator is therefore something which penetrates all. It is not merely a recurring integer, to be detected in any multiple, but a fundamental element which gives consistency and meaning to the whole. It is what has persisted through a process of change where everything else is eliminated. And it has persisted because it is the essential in the process. So, in spite of its inadequacy as a description of any one religion, this constant element — the historical definition — really offers us a clue to the understanding of the entire field.

Fortunately students are agreed upon the elements that are constant; they are, in the last analysis, two, *emotion* and *mystery*. Religion, in the most general terms, is the reaction of mankind to something apprehended but not comprehended. It involves two distinct elements: the object which stimulates, and the psychic life which responds. The response in its keenest form is fear. The ancients made no more profound discovery than that "fear created the gods." But the religious reaction is more than simple fear. It is rather the sense of acceptance than that of escape which is uppermost. Almost every definition of religion — and there are as many as there have been students of it — insists upon this element of acceptance. The essential religious emotion is reverence, which is a compound of fear and appreciation. The word itself reflects this double attitude. It has lost the sense of dread in its root "vereor." It had already lost it in Latin, perhaps because the sense of dread does not readily last over into nouns, but tends to work itself off in a verb. In "reverentia" a new and softer note intervenes, for which we have invented a verb "revere." Blank fear is gone, and we are treasuring the thrills instead, in a tangle of emotions. There is a feeling toward the mystery rather than away from it, an attempt to appropriate all the emotional stimuli it can impart, to absorb its mystic power, — in short, to "worship" it. Religion, then, from savage to civilized, has this in common, that it is, on the one hand, the state of feeling awakened in a man by the sense, in and around him, of mysteries, and, on the other hand, those feelings, actions, customs, and thoughts which that sense produces, and which serve to bring him into relation to them. These things are essentials, as much in the modern world as in the origins of civilization. This is the statement in most general terms of what all of us think of as religion. It leaves the place for secularization by its side; for it resides in the supernatural — or its equivalent. It is a thing of feeling rising into faith on the one hand, and of nervous reactions on the other rising into cult. It is also a social, not an individual, thing. Its ceremonies are weighted with memories of things none of us have ever known, stamped with the mark of an authority that lies beyond the reach of history, and solemn with the wistful outlook of all humanity.

"Mystery" and "emotion" — are these all? Then the historical definition does not seem to define anything; it is inadequate to express the content of any religion known to us — even the most primitive. "Mystery" is a weak word to characterize the object of worship in any stage of society. Why not say "God" or "gods"? With us, certainly, the final test for religion has been, throughout the ages, the belief in God; and anthropology supplements the evidence of history. From fetishes and ghosts to the high divinities of paganism, the world of mystery is peopled with supernatural beings, — whose worship is religion. Indeed, so general is this belief throughout the world that many students of comparative religion have made it, in one form or another, the test for all religions, accepting as satisfactory the definition of E. B. Tylor, the pioneer anthropologist in this field, that the essence of religion is "a belief in spiritual beings." Tylor showed, by a vast survey of savage customs and beliefs, how the primitive mind "animizes" the phenomena of nature; sees spirits and spooks on every hand; imagines life in things that move, elusive spirits in things that startle, ghosts in the dark on windy nights, fairies in the wood, eerie presences in caves, rocks, rivers, etc. These animistic forces form, so Tylor claimed, the background of religion. As society advances it clarifies and modifies these primitive conceptions; the gods change with changes in culture; ultimately one god replaces many. Yet throughout the whole process of evolution, some conception of divinity seems constant.

But recent study has opened up strata more profound than these, at the very foundations of religion. Deeper than gods or demons lies the power in the uncanny itself. Just as the ideas of spirits, gods, and demons clarify themselves with developing civilization from mythology to theology, so the farther back we go the less clear they are, until, at the savage end of the process, they sink into a confused mass in which the sense of individuality tends to disappear. At our civilized end of the process the intellect embodies its religious faith in the conception of God; in the world of the primitive, the senses register the thrills from things uncanny merely in terms of their uncanniness. To be sure, no people has been found where this sort of religious protoplasm has not already produced its spirits; but then no really primitive people exists for our analysis. The savage at his lowest is fairly well developed toward the civilized. But there is abundant evidence of the rôle of this potency of the mysterious quite apart from any idea of spirits, — the "poison" of the sorcerer's spell, the power of the curse or blessing, the "luck" that lies in the uncanny, the "medicine" of the medicine man, which resides in crystals and hocus-pocus, and the like. One may sometimes even watch the spirits emerging from this religious base; first as qualities of it, a differentiation of the particular use or direction of this or that uncanniness; then developing names from adjectives that describe to nouns that "name" as well as describe; and finally receiving genuine worship instead of magical ceremonies. Such, for instance, were those Roman deities mentioned in the first lecture, gods and goddesses of nooks and crannies in house and field, and of the dangers and joys of the farmer's life. The *numina* become divinities. And there is trace of such *numina* throughout the length and breadth of savagery, less spirits than presences, less presences than power. The evidence for this mysterious potency is not absolutely universal, but it is at hand from so much of the savage world as to indicate its universality. It has been detected among people in every quarter of the globe, — in Australia, Africa, America, among Esquimaux, South Sea Islanders, and Hindoos.

We shall get nowhere in the problem before us unless we can appreciate this primal stuff. We must, as it were, put our eyes to the microscope to see the protoplasm of religion, as the biologist studies the embryology

THE PROBLEM AND THE DATA 107

of life. And to do this we must learn to "think savage." We must renounce our civilization, get rid, for a while, of the very mental training which makes our observation possible. We must feel rather than think, or think only so far as feeling urges us. There is no logical system of thought, no vast conception of a primitive philosophy for us to learn. We must, on the contrary, divest ourselves of all that has clarified our impressions into reasoned systems of intelligence, and merge all our thrills into one vague sense of mysterious power.

Imagine that by some potent wizardry these college walls should disappear along with the arts and sciences which have found in them a home. We are savages, camping by the whispering pine grove yonder, with our little patch of corn below against the southern hillside and the great forest belt stretching unbroken beyond it to the blue notched circle of the mountains. We go fishing in the river in the lazy spring days, spearing pike with our stone-chopped arrows, and when not on the warpath against the Iroquois to the west or on the hunt through the river jungle, pass our time in rather monotonous idleness—except, of course, for the work done by the women, which does not matter.

Now the missionaries of the white men report that we have a great spirit, "Manitou," whom we worship. But that is not so. Manitou in Algonkin is originally an adjective, the attribute of mysterious things or beings. It later may develop into a noun, and so may stand for the mysterious things or beings themselves. But it is not an Indian name for God. The sizzling stone in the sweat lodge is manitou, for its steaming potency drives out rheumatism. So are the owl that hoots by the river-path and the wolf that howls from the graveyard. Above all, things seen or heard in dreams are manitou, for they are revelations. There is no distinction between subject and object; the beaver in a dream reveals something, and both the dream-beaver and his revelation are manitou. In short, whenever we experience a mysterious thrill we know that manitou is there. In the words of an Algonkin, who was one of the most brilliant anthropologists America has produced, William Jones, "It is futile to ask an Algonkin [he is speaking of the central tribes] for an articulate definition of the substance [of manitou], partly because it would be something about which he does not concern himself, and partly because he is quite satisfied with only the sentiment of its existence. He feels that the property is everywhere, is omnipresent. The feeling that it is omnipresent leads naturally to the belief that it enters into everything in nature; and the notion that it is active causes the mind to look everywhere for its manifestations." [1]

Manitou is most keenly appreciated at certain sacred times and places. Just as with the civilized the thrill comes surest when the mind is in its most receptive mood. Christians stimulate their sense of mystery by music, by church worship with its age-long association and its subduing touch of silence. So with the Indian. He has his meeting-house for worship, too, where the manitou is doubly real because of the solemn suggestion of time and place.

"The ceremonial lodge is a holy symbol; it means a place where one can enter into communication with high powers, where, with sacrifice and offering, with music and dance one obtains audience and can ask for things beyond human control; it means a place where

[1] *Journal of American Folk-Lore*, vol. xviii, pp. 183–190.

one can forget the material work and enjoy the experience of that magic spell which one feels is the sign that not only is one in the presence of the supernatural property, but in that of the beings who hold it in high degree. It is a function with a very definite purpose. It is to invoke the presence of an objective reality; the objectified ideal may be animate or inanimate. And the effect is in the nature of a pleasing thrill, a sense of resignation, a consolation. This effect is the proof of the presence of the manitou.

"It has thus been observed that there is an unsystematic belief in a cosmic, mysterious property which is believed to be existing everywhere in nature; that the conception of the property can be thought of as impersonal, but that it becomes obscure and confused when the property becomes identified with objects in nature; that it manifests itself in various forms; and that its emotional effect awakens a sense of mystery; that there is a lively appreciation of its miraculous efficacy; and that its interpretation is not according to any regular rule, but is based on one's feelings rather than on one's knowledge." [1]

[1] *Journal of American Folk-Lore, ubi sup.*

This is manitou. Now, let us return from our Mohican village to the Amherst which supplants it to-day. We, too, have our manitou. We call it "grace." The word is almost as elusive in its meaning to us as its Indian counterpart; it is colorless and vague. Although a noun, it is nearly always used as an attribute, in adjectival connection with the divinity. "Grace" by itself means next to nothing; it is completely subordinated to the idea of God. No one would ever suspect from its obscure place in modern theology that it is older than all theologies. It is only in the light of comparative religion that one can see its real significance in religious evolution. It is not risking much now to hazard the hypothesis that it is more fundamental than any idea of spirits, good or evil; nay, more, that it is apparently the source from which they spring, and so the very parent of our idea of God. The potency of the mysterious is the fundamental historical basis of religion.

This opens up a field which we cannot explore farther here — the evolution of the idea of God. The history of that evolution is slowly and surely being recovered; but it lies apart from the perspectives before us. For — to return to our point — the idea of deity is not an essential, or rather let us say a constant, element in religion. Religion is wider than theologies, wider even than a "belief in spiritual beings." It begins with an emotional thrill, an apprehension of things by way of feelings, before the intellect translates these experiences of phenomena into concepts. It therefore begins before the idea of god or demon, because it begins before any ideas at all. It comes out of deeps unplumbed by primitive intelligence, beyond all systems of thought, where emotion is stimulated by a sense of something which is not understood, — where mystery exerts its potency.

Now this is not reducing everything in religion to nothing. Mystery is no mere negative, not even from the standpoint of knowledge. It is not the unknown, nor the unknowable, but simply the un-understood. It is the apprehended but not comprehended, that which is known by sense, intuition, feeling, or whatever you will, but is not made over into full and rational consciousness. We know or rather accept its reality, but we do not know of what that reality consists. It is what the senses register, but the intellect does not master or interpret to itself — except as mystery. Its language is thrill, but thrill is after all a language, and a most effective one. It forces us to listen. The very essence of mystery is that it should obtrude itself upon us and compel our recognition, and yet elude any further revelation of what it is. When we find out what it is, it is no longer a mystery.

The thrill from the mysterious is, therefore, the first phenomenon of religion. But it is something more. Thrill is stimulation, and the emotions that are awakened are the nurseries of thought. The reaction extends beyond the stirring of feelings; it sets going the motor forces of the whole psychic world. The potency in the un-understood, from the savage sense of danger in the uncanny to the Christian experience of the grace of God, has been the main generating, creative element in the evolution of thought, as well as the awakener of emotion. It has, therefore, been the major stimulus in both religion and science.

This is a sweeping statement, and I may not be able to make my meaning entirely plain in the short space at my disposal. But this much is clear, that the mystery is the unappropriated, — that which has not been taken under our control, nor lost to sight in the commonplace. It is the new, the queer, something out of the ordinary, something which provokes attention and continues to provoke it without going deeper into consciousness. It is therefore that part of the environment — material or imaginary, it does not matter — which has intruded and still intrudes itself upon us in the long process of adjustment which makes up the history of our psychic evolution — *and forces the adjustment*. Mysteries are like the jutting crags which bar the pathways of our lives, before which we, as clumsy travelers on a perilous quest, find our hearts sink and our nerveless muscles suddenly beyond control; but which may, just as well, suggest to a bolder spirit a higher and firmer path with larger vistas upon the barrier itself.

We meet our mysteries, then, in either of two attitudes — so long as we meet them at all. One, which has been universally regarded as the religious, is more or less passive. It accepts the thrill, interpreting it in its own terms, which are those of emotion. The other, the scientific, questions. Sometimes it denies the mystery; finds that there is only the shadow of an obstacle in the path instead of an obstacle itself. Sometimes it accepts, frankly confessing that it cannot understand. Whether it understands or not makes relatively little difference, however, for science is to be recognized less by results than by its method and aims.

This distinction of attitudes carries us into the heart of that most persistent of all controversies in this most controversial field, the warfare between religion and science. For the fundamental thing is the contrast in attitudes. Science has no sure and positive results to offer in the place of the absolutes of religion. Its proudest achievements are, in the eyes of metaphysics, art products, like the theologies they displace. There is in the last analysis only a degree of difference between the apprehended and the comprehended. Knowledge itself is mystery. Ether and atoms are myths. No one knows what reason is. Truth is but a relative thing, and scientific laws but the harmony of evidence about phenomena. But whatever strictures philosophy may pass upon the *conclusions* of science, as merely relative and provisional, there is no clearer fact in the history of thought than that its *attitudes* and *methods* have been at opposite poles from those of religion. It does no good to blink the fact, established as it is by the most positive proofs of history and psychology. Science has made headway by attempting to understand the ununderstood, which means attempting to eliminate mystery so far as it can. Religion, on the other hand, has stressed the mystery and accepted it in its own terms. Science is the product of bold adventure, pushing into the realm of the mysterious to interpret its phenomena in terms of the investigator; religion enters this same realm to give itself up to the emotional reactions. Science is the embodiment of the sense of control; religion yields the control to that power which moves in the shudder of the woods by night and the glory of the morning hills.

Many books have been written upon the warfare between religion and science; just as many are written to reconcile the two. They are in the same shop-windows, side by side. One can imagine that some future historian of these ancient times of ours — when we are one with Babylon — may find in them, if any should survive, precious sources for the baffled outlook of our age. Their very contradictions will help him to reproduce the confused horizons of this age of scientific dawn and religious revolution. But he will find little in them except such historic evidence; they will settle no problems for him. Their futility lies in their very nature, for they are mainly written to discuss results, contrasting or comparing the conclusions of science with those of theology. Dealing with the conclusions of to-day, they will be useless to-morrow; they will be antiquarian material for history, but solve no problems of the future; for the data will have changed, and not less in religion than in science.

It would be vastly different, however, if such works were to deal with methods instead of with results, contrasting and comparing the attitudes of science with those of religion. For these are not subject to revision with every change of data. The major attitudes of religion are emotional; those of science intellectual. There is intellectual effort in religion, to be sure, but it is secondary to the emotional. We are often confused upon this point. Simply because theology deals with religion is no reason for regarding it as always religious. Criticism is an attitude of science, not of religion — religion in the historic sense at least. Reverent criticism may fall within the realm of religion, but it is the reverence which makes it religious, not the criticism. Religion accepts the mystery, treasures the thrills. Science moves into the mystery's very heart, and it recognizes no taboos. It is even so intent upon its problem of understanding that it often fails to understand simply on that account, — failing to sympathize emotionally where its classifications of logic do not apply.

Now we come back to our problem — the religious revolution of to-day, and the attempt to appraise it. It is clear that the revolution cannot be measured, since it is more fundamental than the results indicate — momentous as they already are. There is more involved than a conquest of nature by the forces of science; there is a new outlook into the universe, a new attitude toward everything. We are not merely restating the mystery of life and matter for ourselves, we are restating it in terms of change itself, to meet the demands of every new discovery. Truth is no longer a light planted in eternal principles and shining from the past upon our path, where our own shadows cast their weird figures on the dark before us. We carry it ourselves; it moves with us, and its horizons are our own.

We cannot measure such an advance, for it moves with all the potentialities of mankind. But we can indicate its nature and its direction. The more we examine them, the more fundamental the change appears. It is no temporary phase of human interest, soon to be satiated. Knowledge awakens curiosity and curiosity achieves more knowledge. There is no stopping-place in such a process, for the greater the knowledge, the more it reveals its own littleness; and in its sense of ignorance lies the impulse to still more knowledge.

The scientific movement — although still an affair of individuals rather than of society as a whole — is thus cutting in on habits of mind and thought that go back to the animal world — back to the origins of life. It is a revolution in which thought itself is winning its emancipation. Mysteries do not hold back the movement of science; they invite its curiosity and stimulate its activity. Science advances with that high courage which has learned, in the noble words of Lamartine, to make its obstacles its stepping-stones.

"S'appuyer sur l'obstacle et s'élancer plus loin."

But where have we left religion? We carried its origins back to the nerves of primitive adjustment, and made it a sort of sentient register of the first long phases of the evolution of the mind. But is that all? Is it only a thing of low intelligence, to be discarded when the reason begins its reign? Is the revolution that *culbute générale* which Carlyle depicted in the French Revolution? Or has the old régime anything which reason will preserve? These are some of the questions fronting us in the next lecture.

IV

THE NEW REGIME

THERE is a world-old, world-wide belief that a snake can charm its victims. I have been warned in crossing a field, where rattlesnakes were supposed to be hidden in the grass, not to stop and look when I heard a rattle, for if I once saw the snake, it would have me in its power; I should be under its spell and paralyzed while it came up and stung me at its own sweet will. Men of good moral character have assured me that they have seen this done, with chickens, rabbits, and even children; and they had only escaped themselves by carefully avoiding looking at the snake if it was coming toward them!

Now so venerable and universal a belief has something behind it. There *is* some kind of "spell" in the power of the snake; you realize it imaginatively as you listen to the old farmer's story. You have a feeling that you might very well find yourself unable to move when suddenly confronted with so direct and terrible a danger. People will continue to believe in the "spell" of a snake so long as they are likely to be "spellbound" when they see it moving in the grass. It is the property of any such dangers to transfix those who witness them. Ghosts may do this as well as snakes. How generally in ghost stories the victim is "transfixed with horror," his muscles rigid or beyond control, while his eyes are riveted in a hypnotic sort of stare upon the gruesome or terrible objects before him.

Every one knows how art has fastened upon this principle in its tragedies and novels. And there is no more convincing illustration of its application than in the popularity of the sensational journals, with their story of crime in all its ghastly detail. There is a fascination in these things the amount of which can almost be measured by statistics as over against the interest in less gruesome and more normal news. Every civilized country has now its yellow press, and everywhere its circulation is millions larger than that of the sober journals which omit the horrors. Why? Because horror exerts a greater attractive force than reason. Even the staid old journals print what startling news they have with heavier headlines than the more ordinary material, and many a time

I have seen a most well-intentioned man on his way home in the Subway, with a respectable journal under his arm, looking out of the corner of his eye at the grisly columns spread before his more simple-minded and primitive neighbor.

We cannot escape the fact that danger exerts its spell upon us, as it does upon the lower animals. In its intenser forms it can transfix with horror; in its milder, it can fascinate. Often it awakens the combative instinct which nerves us up to face it; just as often it induces flight. But always it attracts attention, and attracts it in proportion to its extent and imminence. Even if we turn our backs and run, it follows and haunts the imagination. The spell of the Ancient Mariner is good on land or sea. Every one knows what it means to have been

> "Like one, that on a lonesome road
> Doth walk in fear and dread,
> And having once turned round walks on
> And turns no more his head:
> Because he knows a frightful fiend
> Doth close behind him tread."

So long as we are in the presence of danger, either imaginatively or really, it absorbs our attention, to the obliteration of other things. Life seems to concentrate its nerves and hold their diverging impressions to a single point. We *are* under a spell.

What is loosely called "the instinct of self-preservation" gathers in and focuses upon one point the whole sentient apparatus of the body. To one "fighting-mad" as to one "spellbound," there is only one thing in the world — the thing of attack or danger. He sees, hears, and feels nothing but it.

None of us remembers exactly what we do in such crises, because our attention is fixed outside of ourselves. We act "instinctively" rather than consciously. This being the case, we can get a better clue to our own behavior at such times by watching animals rather than men, where instinct is more directly at work and less modified by anything approaching purpose. Take a dog barking at the snake, or at anything he scents danger in, a fluttering shadow even. It arouses and holds his attention, and holds it just as it does ours; and like ours it is keenest under such circumstances. The greater the fear, the more intense the attention. So long as the danger is imminent and moves in upon him, his whole being responds, in a fever of excitement; his hair bristles, his body is in a quiver of animation, muscles tense, and every sense on the *qui vive*.

Now let us attempt a rough, psychological analysis of what, to all appearances, happens in such cases. At the climax of excitement one may detect two main reactions, a recoil and a return. If the danger is *too* dangerous, the dog merely recoils and does not come back at it; whines away, beaten in spirit, to hide in safety. But where there is a chance of fight or the vital impulse is strong, the thing of fear draws the dog back to it. He stops his recoil and plunges back to regain his ground. Combativeness shows itself in such instances as the expression of an exuberant life-instinct which has been stung into action by the crisis. Most healthy animals — unless specialized for flight — respond to the note of danger with a note of defiance. It draws them back to face the thing which drives them away. So we have a sort of contradiction in conduct — two opposing impulses forcing backward and forward, the sense of danger and the vital impulse, whatever that may be.

But there is a third possible reaction to a

crisis, neither running away from it nor up to it; just standing still — the reaction exemplified in our own experiences with snakes or — sometimes — mice. It begins with a recoil, but the recoil is held; not returned upon. We do not plunge back to fight, but remain "rooted to the spot," while attention rivets the senses to the object that has startled them. In its extreme form this is blank panic, and lower in point of vital resistance than flight. It is the least thing one can do. But it has possibilities which flight has not, for nine times out of ten the danger is unreal, and by standing still one can learn it, whereas we never know if we run. In such a case, as soon as the panic recedes, we find ourselves played upon by the two opposing desires, danger forcing the recoil and life maintaining us at our post. When the panic does not supervene, or is obliterated, there is recovery in mid-motion, the vital forces holding us up to front the uncanny movements in the grass or the shadow in the moonlight. Still thrilling, we stand, with caught breath, uncertain what to do — and do nothing but look and listen.

What is the relation of all this to the history of religion, and especially to the history of the religious revolution? It is fundamental. For in such crises, where the psychic life shows itself, as it were, in the open, we can see the bases of two major attitudes of the human mind, the fear, awe, and reverence which make for religion, and the curiosity which makes for science. This opens up too vast a subject for satisfactory treatment in this lecture; but I may indicate, in a word, its main lines and their significance.

In the first place, let us review our illustration as a whole. If we have been in the presence of danger — not too dangerous — and yet escaped, we enjoy the experience, if we are healthy beings. We sometimes refer to this as a love of danger; but what we enjoy is, of course, not danger but the stimulation which it gives us. We enjoy the thrill of quivering nerves. The combative instinct is probably but a heightened sense of this, a mastering desire for the extremest form of excitement. Vital force gets the upper hand and carries the fighter along with what he calls "the joy of battle." One can see this in animals as well as in men. I have seen a squirrel jump back and forth from the lower boughs of a tree, apparently to tease a dog, barking furiously, almost within reach below, when the slightest misleap meant death. And the squirrel was chattering its emotional explosions almost as loudly as the dog. Much of our play seems to have begun in such leaps with death; and its charm is largely still in the mimicry of such surprises and escapes.

In milder forms and in infinite variety of incident and expression, this same emotional appreciation of stimulation shows itself on through the developing intelligence of mankind. Art has perpetuated some of its keener and finer forms; and, as we saw at the opening of the lecture, it dominates the widest literature of the present day, our journalism.

Now this emotional appreciation of the stimuli, this treasuring of the thrills which sting the psychic life into its new activity, is the basis of the religious attitude. It is a sort of emotional apprehension of the whole experience of life when penetrated with the keenest stimuli. It is the total reaction of the organism to the dangers or crises which front it. It includes the recoil and the return, the startled movement of alarm and the fascination which keeps us at the danger's brink.

The sense of fear is caught in mid-course and played upon by the cross-currents of vital power; and in that counter-movement, where, as it were, life projects itself upon the avenues of death, or holds itself alert and tense before the spectacle of things beyond control, we have the origins of awe and reverence. Fear transforms itself from a mere alarm for flight to a thrill accepted, enjoyed, and sought after.

Now we turn to the other element in our problem, the curiosity which underlies science. It is clear, to any one who watches a dog in the circumstances just sketched, that curiosity is already in evidence. It, too, like the bases of the religious attitude, goes back to the realm of instinct. Some psychologists call it an instinct in itself; but, as exhibited in such crises, it seems to be rather a part of the general psychic reaction — that part which is at work when the vital impulse checks the recoil and turns us back to see what it is all about. Whether the vital impulse is strong enough to attack the object of fear or only leads us to examine, as in the case of the dog that scratches and sniffs, we exhibit the attitudes of curiosity so long as attention is aroused and keen.

We can carry back, then, to the simple

sensing of things in the animal world, that spirit of inquiry which brings us the achievements of modern science; just as we can carry back the emotions of religion to the elemental response to the stimuli of shock. But note that while the emotions of religion include the whole reaction of the entire psychic life, — not only recoil and return but the pleasure in their interplay, — the sense of curiosity is, at the origins, but a small part of the operation as a whole. Compared with that reservoir of thrills which persists in the emotions of awe or reverence, curiosity seems but a poor thing. And yet, when we look deeply, we find that it, too, has, even at the start, the most tremendous implications. For it is the keenest expression of that attention which is at the basis of knowledge.

There is a familiar conundrum in chemistry, How do hydrogen and oxygen unite so as to become water? The answer is, that they do not *become* water; they *produce* it. For water is different from its elements. So, it will be claimed by some, in this experiment in psychology, even if these emotions of shock are the elements which produce religion, they are not religion itself; any more than curiosity is science. This line of argument has been followed by some to deny altogether the value of any such genetic study of behavior as we are embarked upon. They claim that just as we could never tell from hydrogen or oxygen alone the properties of H_2O, or water, so we get no clue as to the real nature of modern religion by analyzing it into its constituents.

The obvious answer to this is that if the science of psychology can get upon a line of analysis as fruitful as those of chemistry and physics, we shall at least "know" its phenomena as well as we know anything else. Whether shock and thrill become religion or produce it, one thing is sure, there is no religion without their action. They run in a constant line through the whole series of religious phenomena, from the lowest up. Is this without significance? Certainly not. The flaw lies in the analogy. We should compare religion, not with gases or chemical elements, but with the phenomena of life. The biologist will admit that the conundrum holds in his field as well as in physics — but will add at once that it does not cover the whole ground. The microscope reveals the process of growth as one in which new cells are added to old, old give way to more new, and so on. It is a process of production and reproduction. Our bodies change minute by minute, breath by breath. The old does not become the new; it makes it, brings in new chemicals, new tissues, new organisms. But, on the other hand, from the standpoint of their functioning and substance, the organisms remain what they were. For in the processes of vital change there remains an essential sameness. The great law of growth — that law which is the baffling puzzle of biology to-day — makes the new like the old. Ontogeny repeats phylogeny. So, in those sciences which deal with life, it is not so misleading as the critic thinks, to say that one thing becomes another instead of making it.

To be sure, a knowledge of the elements of religion in savages does not furnish one with a description of its potentialities in civilized society, any more than a knowledge of unicellular organisms describes the human frame. But after all it is through the unicellulars that we first come to know whatever we do know of the secret of growth and the functions of the complex organs of the multicellulars. It was the discovery of bacteria which first made possible a scientific treatment of the body. In the same way the science of religion must apply its results. And I venture the opinion, from a survey of the field to-day, that it is destined to produce as radical a reconstruction in the understanding and treatment of religion as took place in the science of medicine when bacteriology replaced the semi-magical quackery of herb-doctors and leeches.

As I said before, we are not dealing with the theological problem of the reality of God, but with the historical and psychological data of how men react. We are concerned with the *attitudes* of religion and science, rather than with their conclusions. Now the attitude changes with a change in knowledge; and this fact, which, in the realm of metaphysics, is the pragmatic justification of knowledge, is, in the practical realm before us, the secret of the religious revolution. For what we have at present is a lessening of the emotional appreciation of mystery and a strengthening of the curiosity which leads toward science. We have seen the rudiments of both the emotion and the curiosity in the realm of instinct; we must now trace their action in the complex world of rational consciousness.

Religion, I repeat, is a development from that sensing of shock which is already seen in the animal world. It is a thing of crises and mystery, when the psychic life is stirred by some major stimuli and responds in thrill. Religion is born of that emotional state which includes all of these things, — the sense of the mystery or the thing of shock, on the one hand, and on the other the vital impulse which goes out to meet it, — sympathetically. It is the total emotional appreciation of both stimuli and reactions; and we may give it the name religion so soon as that appreciation is registered in consciousness. The stimulus comes in from without. It is outside of the horizon of the understood, and its generic name is "mystery." The major response is the fear which is held in poise by the power of life's resistance, — that is to say, fear transmuted into awe and reverence.

I have already said this several times over. But now let us follow up the implications. There are two which follow directly. In the first place, we must admit the reality of the stimulus in mystery, and in the second, the value of it.

The reality of the stimulus is proved by the

reaction. There *is* a power in mystery and danger which can quicken the whole psychic life. Whatever the reason may think of it later, the emotions accept that reality and act upon it. Reason may even prove that there is no danger and that the mystery is a delusion, but so long as the emotions register a thrill there is a reality — for them. In the realm of sensation, whatever thrills, is. Indeed the thrill may be heightened instead of lessened by the denial of its legitimacy by the reason. Such experiences carry one into the very heart of mystery itself, — which from the standpoint of reason is simply the un-understood. The reality of the stimulus, then, is assured by the emotions; it is real to them or they would not thrill. Upon this essential fact religion is based.

This suggests the second point, that of value. The emotions enjoy the thrill and treasure it; and that appreciative valuation is the basis of the idea of the sacred. The sacred is the mysterious, whose potency society has experienced and stressed. It is something known to the emotions, but not to the reason, — except as a phenomenon of emotion. It is recognized by its power, for it is loaded with the stimulus of shock. It can bless or curse, for the sacred in early society may act either way, and even with us a moment's thought will show that the one can never be sure of the direction which the mysterious efficacy of a spell may take. The sacred umbrella of the priestly king blesses its owner and is deadly unlucky to any other who touches or looks at it. The sacred number seven is respected by us, not because of anything that happened on any seventh day, but because Babylonian priests insisted upon its mystic power; the sacred number thirteen, on the contrary, merely curses. The altar of any god in any sacrificial cult has always the same terrible power of taboo. It kills or injures the impure who approach. In fact, the whole religion of sacrifice (*sacrificium*, note the word) is due to this potency in things sacred. It is the art of directing the potency for our benefit instead of for our bane. But whether it hurts or helps, the sacred is the embodiment of the stimulus of shock; and the things in which it resides are those which have not been made over into the commonplace, on the one hand, or so fully explained away by the reason, on the other, as to fail of further recognition even by the emotions.

The sacred, then, lies in essence outside habit and the categories of logic. But in its operation it becomes fundamental in both. For, although in origin they are the unhabitual and unappropriated things which become sacred, — the things of danger and of crisis, — these same things once sacred are always sacred. Emphasizing the thrill tends to exalt it and to perpetuate it. Any attempt upon it is sacrilege; even its examination is sacrilege to a second degree, to be dealt with by society as both sin and crime. For where there is failure to convict and punish openly, we suffer in our consciences, which are the intimate reflection of what others think of us. This very analysis of mine is sure to meet somewhere with just such condemnation, as a violation of sacred truth or mystery. In more primitive society it would bring exile or death. So the sacred not only intrudes within the realm of habit, but resides inviolable in its very heart, safeguarded by all the forces of society. It fastens itself upon us with the power of its original stimulus, strengthened by the unquestioned repetition of all the ages.

This is the secret of the conservatism of religion. As the embodiment of this sense of the sacred, it is the most conservative thing in the world. It perpetuates adjustments begun before the dawn of thought, thrills that show themselves in the behavior of the lower animals. It is not by chance that the Catholic Church has as its motto "Semper idem." That has been the motto of a larger catholicity than any theologian has ever dreamed of — a catholicity that includes every sacred thing and every emotional response in the history of humanity — and beyond. For behind it lies the great law of Habit, — that hidden despot of the whole realm of life. Habit is just unconscious repetition; and repetition is the largest law of Nature itself.

Only by an effort of the conscious will, or by the impulsion of some new, compelling stimulus, can we change our conduct, and do something new. Our lives fit into Nature's repetition, with its recurring days and seasons; our nerves accept equally the silence of the woods or the rhythmic din of the city streets, so long as they continue either silent or filled with noise. But let a single crow call in the fields, or the street suddenly hush its traffic in mid-career, and the mind suddenly becomes aware of silence in the first case, and sound in the second. So long as the perfect succession endured, the mind went on, like Nature, receiving stimuli and letting them go, as we say, in at one ear and out at the other.

This rôle of habit is so tremendous that its very universality makes it hard to see. It extends through the animal creation as definitely as through the field of human society. Indeed, it is more a social than an individual thing. Society sets our habits for us, and engraves the tablets of the law in what we call our consciences. In this way it finds a substitute for what to it is a defect in our biological make-up, — the inability to inherit acquired characteristics. And its substitute is, to say the least, a fair equivalent for the missing inheritance. If birth does not supply us with habits, it supplies us with tendencies for their acceptance. And the habits come before consciousness. A baby will acquire the habit of going to sleep only when one walks with it, before it has learned to localize its bottle, — that first lesson in spatial concepts.

Geologists tell how, in the distant past, the glaciers wore down our hills and grooved our valleys, and then, in the long ages since, the streams have kept wearing ever deeper those same grooves. Palæontologists now tell us that man was here through the whole vast process, and they find his bones of the prehistoric past along those same river drifts, where his cities cluster now. But it remains for the psychologist who examines the geology of behavior, not merely of man but of life as a whole, and not simply of individuals but of society as well, to find that in that inner world of sensations, whose frail contours burst in less cosmic revolutions, the grooves of feeling have been wearing down in the same inevitable and eternal process, until we of to-day, with all our boast of intellectual independence, with a glorious history of emancipation to our credit, are still little more than helpless river-beds for the currents of habitual feeling and conduct. Religion, with its *semper idem*, sanctifies its own stimuli.

Here is the setting for the part played by belief, not simply in religion but in every department of thought. Belief is just the continuance in consciousness of this tendency of nerves and senses to accept and repeat their stimuli. It is only in this light that the full significance of its tremendous rôle in our lives can be appreciated — for so much of it is still beyond the rim of consciousness. It is the nature of our minds to believe, just as it is of our senses to feel. Doubt is an acquisition; belief is born with us. The only things we doubt — naturally — are those which run counter to a previous body of accepted beliefs. The will to believe is as deep as life itself.

It may be objected that I am using the word "belief" too widely, in stretching it to reach outside intellect into the field of emotion. Belief commonly means a conscious mental act; accepting as true something known and tested. When one says "I believe," one stands up mentally before the world to state the result of an inner examination. When the parish priests taught the crude minds of our peasant forefathers the Creed, and they responded in its simple but moving recital, it would seem as if theology were giving mankind its first formal lessons in introspection, and that the result was a mental clarification on the deepest mystery in life. But we are in danger of confusing the belief with its confession on the one hand and its content on the other. Belief in this sense is neither the mystery nor the Creed, but that active principle which makes creeds out of mysteries. This at once sets it forth as wider than intellect. The belief which we are dealing with is no more a purely rational process than the "will" to believe is conscious and rational. The phrase "the will to believe" is, as we have been shown so clearly, a sort of biological expression, indicating the life impulse projected in a certain direction. It is that tendency to accept from the start at face value the impressions which the senses register, simply because that is their business.

But this statement of the all-embracing character of the process of belief furnishes no justification why the reason should accept its conclusions. Indeed, it is the duty as it is the nature of reason to turn back upon this process and challenge it at every step. Reason is the critic which saves belief from credulity and purifies philosophy from myth. There is a fashion nowadays to decry its action. Reason, according to one anthropologist, is only justification for our prejudices. James and Bergson and the pragmatists have beset it around and about. But though hard-pressed by its own offspring, — for presumably this new philosophy is reasonable, — it yet remains the valid critic of our lives. We should be in a bad way if it were not, for it is the only critic we have, — and therefore the only critic of itself. We may not know how far it, too, like the faiths it challenges, is determined from beyond consciousness, by the same influences which render them untrustworthy; we may have little more confidence in its conclusions than in the simple blunderings they replace. We may even not know just what it is. But we can see its results in a new heaven and a new earth and read its justification in the glory of that rational control, which extends out into time and space, and plants there the empire of the mind, — which extends back into the motive forces of life and society and turns them to new and loftier ideals. I have no doubt but that reason will profit from this very movement of philosophic anti-rationalism which dominates today, and, chastened by a statement of its limitations, — which, like all schoolmasters it has been slow to admit, — move with a truer step into the heart of that pervading mystery which is the stimulus of science as of religion.

Now, reason, as I have said, is not able to accept the conclusions of belief unless it has had a chance to verify or test their truth. It is never — when it is itself — overawed by the sense of authority. It recognizes no authority but its own. Indeed, to the trained mind, which has learned to look back upon itself and has had a glimpse of the power of emotion and its vagaries in our lives, there is nothing more suspect than the conclusions of a universal belief. The catholic appeal to what all men have believed, everywhere, at all times, is just what the psychologist is least sure of. For the conclusions contained in such ancient creeds embody that untrained, unrational appreciation of mystery which thrilled into primeval brains and passed on into the realm of consciousness as both thrill and thought — the manitou which, in the mind of the Algonkin, plays over both dream-beaver and its revelation. This was the origin of myth. Myth did not begin as an explanation of mystery but as its statement, when the shocks of the emotions were translated over into the language of thought. Thought phrased them as a story; but so unclarified was the mind in which that story lay, that subject and object, cause and effect, were all confused. One can see examples of this in any myth. Aurora is both the dawn and the dawn angel, just as manitou is the power in the mystery and the mystery itself. There is no logic of cause and effect because the emotions apprehend by the effect alone and do not know the cause except as apart from the result. The Indians of New Guinea say that more people are drowned in the rapids of their rivers than in the more tranquil stretches, *because* the spell of those already drowned makes the rapids drown others. There is a truth in this for the emotions, — as in the case of the snake. But reason does not, for all that, accept the existence of the demons of the rapids, as myth goes on to interpret the situation.

Myth is the embodiment, in the form of a story, of the experiences of shock, and comes frankly from the realm of the un-understood. It conveys the impression of the mystery it describes. One recites it with lower breath, by midnight fires, in sacred places. It carries conviction by arousing a repetition of the original emotions which called it into being. But in the eyes of reason it is no satisfactory record of reality. Reason says it must be given up.

Its untrustworthy character is now stamped in the very word itself. Yet religion has been describing its mysteries in terms of myth throughout all history. The myths themselves become sacred, from the very weight which society puts upon them. Creeds tend to become sacramental, carrying with them, like the substance of baptism or eucharist, the miraculous power of the mystery which they embody in thought.

Now we are in danger again of confusing the content of a belief with the function of believing. It is absolutely fundamental to remain clear upon this point, and, in order to emphasize it by well-known things, I shall venture for a moment into Christian theology. Christianity has emphasized faith as perhaps no other religion. Modern scholarship now claims that this emphasis was due rather to the insistent pressure of Greek than to purely Jewish elements. But "justification by faith" did not mean, to Paul or to Luther, the subscription to a few set conclusions. It was and is much more than the acceptance of a myth — and much of what both believed was mythical. It is that emotional attitude toward mystery which accepts and treasures it, and interprets in terms of that acceptance. It is, as it were, the ecstasy of reverence, the joy in fear. This is something older than Greek or Jew, older than all theologies. The faith which justifies is as wide as the experience of all mankind and reaches back to the dawn of thought. Its exact content, on the other hand, has no such universal sanction. On the contrary, it is never the same in any two believers. The substance of the faith of Paul not only was different from that of Luther, but it varies with every brain which mirrors in fleeting impression the faint, blurred facts of history.

We cannot follow this line where it would lead us. But from the point already reached, we can now see the religious revolution of to-day in a new and clearer light, — and I venture to add, in a more tremendous and impressive form. For now we can realize what is the significance of that change in attitude upon which it depends. Science does not justify by faith, but by works. It is the living denial of that age-long acceptance which we accord the mystery — as such. It renounces authority, cuts athwart custom, violates the sacred, rejects the myths. It adjusts itself to the process of change whose creative impulse it itself supplies. Not *semper idem*, but *semper alterum* is the keynote of science. Each discovery of something new involves the discarding of something old. Above all, it progresses by doubting rather than by believing. The first thing the historian must learn is to doubt his sources, refuse to believe his authorities. It was by such denial in the cities of Ionian Greece that history, as distinguished from myth, came into existence, when the forerunners of Herodotus grew skeptical about the stories of Homer. And it was the absence of this skepticism which has made the mediæval chronicler an object of contempt. Science recognizes no "authorities"; it tests everything. It has no creeds, but only working hypotheses; even its laws of gravitation are being recast at the present moment. No sacredness inheres in its ideas; the older they are the less we rely upon them, for the mechanism of observation and experiment is perfecting as we go, and the earlier scientists could often only guess where we can measure and weigh. So here, too, the attitude is the reverse of that seen in the treasuring of religious faith. Moreover, philosophy has caught the tone of science, and carries the doubt beyond where the scientist generally would carry it. For when science ventures to place in its own discoveries the confidence which it refuses to the unscientific world, metaphysics and psychology combine to show that the so-called "facts" of chemistry or biology are myths like those they replace. Everything is relative; absolutes disappear. The very philosophy which has given consolation to mystics by its attack upon reason, carries us logically to the heart of pessimism. Knowledge is never sure, — truth is never quite apprehended. In short, the mystery is too much for us.

The religious revolution now stands before us in all its red Jacobinism. It is part of a vast movement which invades every field of thought. Viewed from the position we have now reached in our survey, it appears as the transference of our ideals from a world of faith to one of doubt, from myth to rationalism, acceptance to denial. Are we, then, heading for that "Everlasting No" which Carlyle so graphically described three quarters of a century ago? Is there nothing left us but the fleeting vision of phenomena, whose reality forever lies beyond our ken? So at least it seems to many an observer, and especially to those who watch the movement from the high places of philosophy. For instance, in a book published recently, Professor Santayana's "Winds of Doctrine," we are told that the intellectual temper of our age is one in which "our whole life and mind is saturated with the slow, upward infiltration of a new spirit — that of an emancipated, atheistic, international democracy." "How," he asks, "should there be any great heroes, saints, artists, philosophers, or legislators in an age when nobody trusts himself or feels any confidence in reason, in an age when the word dogmatic is a term of reproach?"

But now is all this pessimism justified? The red flag of socialism seems to the shuddering bourgeois the symbol of the blood of its victims; to the workers enrolled under it, it symbolizes the common life-blood of a universal brotherhood of man. The grizzly omen of fear and death means really an ideal of life and hope. So it is possible that the revolution which we are analyzing may offer for the onward march some such inspiration out of the very heart of its destructive forces.

One thing is sure, that inspiration must be

found there or not at all. It must be armed with
the strength of the conqueror, not with the
mere protest of defeat. There is no salvation
in that sickly obscurantism which attempts to
evade realities by confusing itself about them.
Safety lies only in clarity and the struggle for
the light. No subliminal nor fringe of consciousness
can rank in the intellectual life beside
the burning focal centre where the rays
of knowledge converge. The hope must lie in
following reason, not in thwarting it. To turn
back from it is not mysticism; it is superstition.
No; we must be prepared to see the higher criticism
destroy the historicity of the most sacred
texts of the Bible, psychology analyze the
phenomena of conversion on the basis of adolescent
passion, anthropology explain the genesis
of the very idea of God. And where we
can understand, it is a moral crime to cherish
the un-understood.

But now let us review our material. First
of all, mystery *does* stimulate; it quickens the
whole psychic life, and as that includes, at our
end of the process, both religion and science,
mystery stimulates both of these. That stimulus
may be treasured in the realm of the emo-

tions, in what we call reverence and awe; and as such a treasure it passes on into the world of clarified impressions as the sacred — still exerting its spell. Myth is its embodiment, though later regarded as its explanation. But the stimulus may also bring out curiosity, which also goes back to the realm of instinct. Curiosity began as an integral part of the primitive psychic reaction, — that part of the reaction in which man ventured to assert himself over against the mystery. It is an expression of the vital impulse, that same vital impulse, which, if I am correct in my analysis, also underlies the transformation of fear into reverence. But here the impulse pushes back to meet the mystery. It is combative, impatient of its stimulus, irritated by it instead of charmed. It is more intent upon other things, most likely upon attaining the solution of its problem, than the beauty of the operation. It tends to be practical rather than poetical. Stressing this side, it naturally tends to lose sight of the mystery and to generate confidence in itself. So it develops a habit of doubt as over against that submission and acceptance which resides in the emotional apprehension.

These two elements of our psychic life, the

one stressing the recoil and acceptance, the other based upon the assertion of will, have gone diverging paths through the history of our intellectual evolution. Their contradictory tendencies have been emphasized and they have been pulled apart. Until to-day their faces have been set in opposite directions — witness the feeling of antagonism, and the literature upon the warfare between religion and science. Science has been so disgusted with the bogies which the emotions have created out of mysterious things that it has little patience with that timorous attitude which awaits the thrill. It is impatient not less because of the unreliable character of such impressions than because of the attitude itself which seems unworthy the dignity of man. Religion, on the other hand, has gone on treasuring its thrills, stressing the sacred, creating myths, explaining its mystery in terms of the un-understood, doing everything, in fact, which science disapproves of.

Now if this is to continue, the outlook is clear. For science is moving the mystery farther and farther from the sphere of daily life and action, destroying taboos, and building up a world of rational experience; and if religion is nothing but the submission to mystery, it is doomed. If it is the trembling register of fear transmuted maybe into softened keys but always fear — pulsating through awe and reverence, with the suggestion of a power beyond control — if this is all there is in life that is religious, it is not enough to satisfy the rational intelligence. Yet that is what a theology based upon the irrational background of life demands. In short, there must be religion of the head as well as of the heart, if the head is getting control of the situation — or else religion will share the fate of the emotions in which it has been enthroned. It will be disbarred from directing the life of intelligence, both individual and social.

It is no answer to decry the head, to insist upon what the rationalist knows only too well, that we are embryos in reason and millenniums old in emotions, and that most of our lives are passed under their authority. For already the emancipation of the intelligence has proceeded far enough for us to see its tremendous possibilities. Science has already justified itself by works. It has made our civilization. It has even found a method by which Nature itself reveals its secrets: experiment replaces expe-

THE NEW REGIME 155

rience, and the forces of the world measure themselves before our eyes.

I do not think the significance of this has yet been sufficiently realized. The new knowledge can be expressed largely in terms of control. We are made masters of atoms and moving tides. We play upon the forces of Nature as the musician upon his piano. Time and space yield to a more powerful witchery than any mythic dream. Reality shapes itself along our path; and we move with growing confidence and power. Nor does this achievement of control have to do only with the material world. It has justified itself in the realm of conduct even more. Morals for us are no longer a set of taboos recording the irrational reactions of past millenniums; they are being taken over by the intelligence of mankind, — and for the first time we are cleaning our moral slums efficiently because we know how. Charity, as I said before, is not now a mystical virtue for the giver, but a business to be looked into from the standpoint of society. In morals as a whole we are growing franker and seeing straighter, and all because we have learnt to displace the heart, in such matters, by the head. It may as well be said once for all, that, young as the intelligence is, it is already sufficiently in control of the situation in social affairs as in material, that any effort to thwart it is going to react disastrously upon whoever and whatever tries to do so.

But there is a larger view than this antagonism; one which carries along into our modern world the general synthesis which we called religion in the primitive, — the *whole* operation in which the mystery was apprehended, both receptivity and curiosity. Throughout untold ages the highest values of life have lain in the emotions which perpetuate the receptivity, — reverence and awe. Curiosity has been secondary and neglected. Now it claims the lead. Hence the religious revolution. In the new régime whose glorious creations are already before our eyes, reason claims our allegiance. Will it discard all but itself? Or will it recognize the legitimacy of emotion as a register of stimuli even while mistaking their origin? Is there no possibility of awe and reverence except in a realm of delusion?

There are two things which make eternally awe and reverence possible. And they are the two which set us going along the whole path of this evolution, from primitives to ourselves — *life*, on the one hand, and *matter*, on the other — and both are mysteries. Life with its "push," its will, its vital impulse, of which science expresses only part; matter into which plays this questioning and emotional force. If both should prove to be but one — if life is a mechanism — it would not change the situation; there would still be two parts of a mystery in play and counter-play. These are final mysteries, and there is no fulcrum in all the universe to move them from our path, however we strain on the lever.

Mankind for untold ages has appropriated these mysteries and their attendant phenomena mainly by emotion — and the result has been stagnation and defeat. Here and there in the long past a little advance was made, reason developing to grapple with mysteries as problems. Elimination of errors brought clarification; magic yielded to worship, spell to prayer, orthodoxies became heresies and heresies superstitions. Religious evolution showed in successive stages a parallel, faint but traceable, to the progress of the secular life. This is what we saw in our first lecture, when we discovered that the religious revolution of to-day is but the last, swift phase of an age-long movement correlative with the rise of civilization. From the standpoint of their own time even the prophets have been lessening, rather than enlarging, the social scope of religion, as they purified it. Purifying meant, generally, getting rid of elements no longer consistent but none the less effective in an unenlightened world. When the prophets of Jahve proclaimed that a pure heart was more acceptable to him than burnt offerings, they struck a blow at a mode of worship as universal as religion itself. It would be like declaring to-day that the churches should be closed. When Jesus cut in so ruthlessly upon the Pharisaical observance of the "law," he violated taboos at every turn. From the standpoint of the Pharisee there was a loss in religion and an intrusion of the secular upon it. So one might run over the history of Christianity, and watch its superstitions wear away in the light of a steadily dawning intelligence. The process is even clearer in the pagan world. One should recall the charge of "atheism" directed against the keenest thinkers of antiquity and the greatest of its moral reformers. But what was personal and incidental in the past, depending largely upon the genius and inspiration of seers and leaders, has now become a social movement, as wide as science. The sphere of emotional play in the realm of mystery is now limited by the dominant reason — is or tends to be. And the result is a knowledge which carries with it control — and the religious revolution.

It is time to close, and yet we have just begun the consideration of that element of our problem which is of most vital interest to us. The past, which held its meaning, and the outer world which reveals it, have kept us too long from ourselves. We must leave for another time and circumstance the application of our investigations in the world of to-day. But we have already seen that this revolutionary era in religion as in science is no temporary phase of the history of thought. The ground which has been won will not yield to the forces of superstition under any disguise of orthodoxy; it is secure for all future time, because the life of civilization has established itself upon them. The gains of Hellenic genius were almost entirely in the realm of thought and art, in the realm of poetry and not of the practical life. Those of Judea were if anything more unpractical still. In fact, practicality has borne a stigma through all the pre-scientific age. It is now the strength of our intellectual emancipation. For the comforts of the body as well as of the mind are to be found in the new régime, and no blind barbarism is able to withstand this double appeal. Science controls as well as studies disease, prevents the dangers its viligance discloses, and stands like a warder along the frontiers of experience. It is increasing the store of wealth and now calling for a higher justice in its distribution. Armed with such powers, it is invincible; the pre-scientific era can no more return than the pre-historic. We left our cave shelters of the frozen past many thousand years ago, built our cities and spread out our nations; but until yesterday — and even now — the mind has kept reverting to those hidden channels where it groped in blindness and marked its spells of magic on the subterranean walls. It does so still whenever it has a chance, *but the chances are lessening*. It is too much to say that the reign of reason is at hand, for most of us are still primitive through and through; but it is not too much to say that the irrational is henceforth doomed to yield up the command of the motive forces of conscious conduct.

The achievements of the intellect have been greater than most people suspect. Its scope is not to be measured by any single discoveries in science or philosophy, but in the general movement toward rational control. Evolution brings emancipation; it offers life the poise that secures judgment upon its actions and dreams, instead of the blind, quick satiation of emotion. The reason is working out a vaster science than we dream of — a *scientia scientiarum* which is not metaphysics or theology, but simply the great science of living. This is not a new creation, for it is as old as thought, but it has only now won its way to the position of control. It does not ignore those old crude impressions which lie behind its intellectual creations. It recognizes the emotions which are stung into being along the quivering nerves, just as definitely as the thoughts which follow. But it knows where to place such phenomena and how to interpret them.

Finally, nothing that is fundamental in our

experience is lost. Indeed, since we now see the mystery in life itself which we used to find in death, as long as life endures the tremulous note of reverence will sound across the still, clear spaces of the mind. But the tone from that eternal thrill will be moulded, under the control of reason, into other forms than that fantastic, barbaric and discordant theme which has held, and still so largely holds, the drama of our ancient myths — and our theologies.

THE END

The Riverside Press
CAMBRIDGE . MASSACHUSETTS
U . S . A